God Is Unconscious

God Is Unconscious

Psychoanalysis and Theology

Tad DeLay

Foreword by Peter Rollins

WIPF & STOCK · Eugene, Oregon

GOD IS UNCONSCIOUS
Psychoanalysis and Theology

Wipf & Stock
An Imprint of Wipf and Stock Publishers
199 W. 8th Ave., Suite 3
Eugene, OR 97401

www.wipfandstock.com

ISBN 13: 978–1–4982–0849–9

Manufactured in the U.S.A.   02/03/2015

In the beginning was the Word,

And the Word was with the Other,

And the Word was the Other.

The Word issued forth from the Other in the beginning.

And the Word entered the world and made humankind from machine,

And we live in the aftermath.

Contents

Foreword

by Peter Rollins

IN 1912 A POLISH book dealer named Wilfred Voynich purchased a mysterious manuscript thought to have been composed in Northern Italy during the Italian Renaissance. The manuscript itself was an obscure, esoteric script composed of approximately thirty-five thousand "words," spread over 240 pages that comprised six sections.

What gave the document its mesmerizing appeal was quite simple: it was a carefully crafted text full of illustrations that no one could understand.

The Latin-esque markings appeared to obey a crude grammar and syntax, yet these seeming signifiers roamed free, defying any stable link to a signified. The Voynich manuscript, as it became known, quickly established itself as one of the most interesting enigmas in cryptography, with experts discussing whether the author was a cryptographer, charlatan, outsider artist, mystic channeling glossolalia, or some poor scholar suffering from a brain trauma.

Like Hopelandic, the invented "language" of Icelandic band Sigur Rós, the Voynich manuscript easily evokes a feeling of meaning, yet this meaning is frustratingly experienced as simultaneously eroded. Something seems to be said, yet this said remains too ethereal to grasp.

Reading Lacan can often evoke the same feeling one gets when encountering the Voynich manuscript, and similar claims have been made about the former as those concerning the author of the latter. Alan Sokal, for example, claimed that Lacan's use of science is utterly nonsensical, while Noam Chomsky has referred to him as a self aware charlatan. For some Lacan is dismissed a master huckster blessed with a gift that enables him to fool some of the smartest people in the room, while for others he's hailed as an indispensable guide for those grappling with the complexity of human subjectivity and the ideological systems which this subjectivity invents/inhabits.

Yet, just like the Voynich manuscript, Lacan's work has, in its resistance to easy interpretation or reduction to a University Discourse, generated a significant industry of academic production. His work continues to have a profound impact in critical theory and has been put to use in all manner of fields from literary studies, feminism, and film theory, to jurisprudence, linguistics, and philosophy. His teachings have not only been productive in generating new concepts and distinctions but have provided ways of challenging the very frame these disciplines use to approach their respective areas of inquiry. The harvest produced by his work is thus found well beyond the field of psychoanalytic practice it was cultivated in. Even for those who wonder whether Lacan's work is meaningful, it cannot be denied that the work is ripe for meaning making.

One of the disciplines that one would expect to have been impacted by the industrious work of Lacanians is that of theology, if for no other reason that Lacan himself often used theological references, quoted theological thinkers, and commented upon a link between the Protestant Reformation and the psychoanalytic revolution. Yet this has, with a few exceptions, not been reflected in the literature.

This situation has been changing in recent years with a new generation of thinkers, partly inspired by Žižek's theological investigations, reflecting on Lacan's corpus with religion in mind. With *God Is Unconscious* Tad DeLay has boldly entered this fray with an important contribution that offers clear coordinates with which to navigate the landscape of Lacan's teaching while also preserving his unique voice. Providing clarity while maintaining Lacan's voice is no easy accomplishment. To err on one side risks turning Lacan's writing into a series of hackneyed sayings, while erring on the other runs the danger of providing a map as baffling as the landscape it outlines. DeLay avoids these pitfalls by providing a brilliant overview of Lacan's work that is disrupted by a wealth of quotes. These quotes are not domesticated by his interpretation but are set alongside his reflections to challenge, deepen, and enrich them.

DeLay provides the reader with a powerful overview for those standing on the threshold of Lacan (which includes those who have read him many times before), but he also puts Lacan's corpus to theological work. More than this he demonstrates how Lacan's teaching impacts the work of theology. This is not a book that mines Lacan's text for explicit theological

Foreword

references or themes; rather it shows how Lacan's overall project disrupts, deepens, and challenges the very field of theological inquiry. DeLay takes seriously Lacan's claim that psychoanalysis and theology are closely linked and draws this out in ways that are clarifying and fruitful.

DeLay has spent years with Lacan's teachings. He has sat with them, worked through them, and let them speak into him. The fruit of that labour is what you hold in your hands, an insightful and fertile text that will prove invaluable for those who wish to grapple with Lacan seriously and theologically.

Those who have spent years traversing Lacan's texts will tell you that endurance is required. It's hard to avoid periods of frustration while reading Écrits or confronting confusion when working through the Seminar. Yet countless people have found their labors rewarded by points of clarity, insight, and productive association. Which brings us to a second requirement: guides to help encourage you and draw your attention to what might otherwise be missed. In *God Is Unconscious* DeLay proves to be such a guide. He doesn't do all the work for us, masticating the food so that we might swallow it without the effort or the taste, but instead he helps make the formidable material more palatable so that we might experience how nourishing it really is.

Introduction

I did not write them in order for people to understand them, I wrote them in order for people to read them. Which is not even remotely the same thing . . . People don't understand anything, that is perfectly true, for a while, but the writings do something to them.[1]

The basic thing about analysis is that people finally realize that they've been talking nonsense at full volume for years.[2]

SAILING INTO NEW YORK Harbor, Sigmund Freud stood on the deck with Carl Jung and gazed out at the statue illuminating the world. Their arrival was a much-anticipated event for American psychologists so very curious of what this new theory of the psyche could expose. Whether out of hubris or prescience—and are they not often one and the same?—Freud turned to his disciple and whispered, "They don't realize we're bringing them the plague."[3]

A psychoanalytic theology is a conception of trauma. Façades of humility and arrogance alike betray the illusions we inflict upon ourselves with an irascible wrath, all for the misguided notion that our trauma will not surface and show itself through the veneer of security. The illusion of non-anxiety works until it does not. Psychoanalysis is concerned with what does not work.[4] In the beginning the signifier entered our world to

1. Lacan, *Triumph of Religion*, 69–70.
2. Lacan, *My Teaching*, 71.
3. Lacan, *Écrits*, 336.
4. Lacan, *Triumph of Religion*, 61.

designate our reference points for identity to which we are always irrevocably attached.

> It is when the Word is incarnated that things really start going badly.[5]

The underside of a signifier's power to tell us who we are contains an ever-present, if only latent, power to construct the most unforgivable narratives. And so in our twenties or thirties we enter therapy to begin to discern what happened to us in our earlier years. We imagine we begin the process for any number of reasons, but really these reasons are all derivatives of two—and ultimately only two—reasons we seek help. First, we feel separated by a constitutive and fundamental lack and suspect we will never be loved, accepted, or known as fully as we wish. Second, our alienation ensures we shall never fully escape our history—the best and the worst experiences mold us in ways beyond our control, and it is profoundly disturbing to realize we are conditioned by elements that have been thrust upon us. We are irrevocably the symptom of the experiences shaping our desire, and we cannot regress to a neutral state of non-conditioned naïveté. Our alienation begins the moment we learn as infants that there rules of the house we are powerless to protest; this trace inscription evolves into an elaborate latticework of self-imposed injunctions that shape our identities. Like the old authoritarian motto—the more you profess your innocence, the more you deserve to be shot—the more we obediently submit to the superego crafted precariously from our parents and friends, our political economies and our books, our demons and our gods, the more we are under its judgment. We live in the aftermath of the signifier's incarnation and adopt our psychopathological dispositions, and we anxiously feel the Gaze of the big Other.

WE SPEAK INDIRECTLY: FROM THE RITUAL TO THE PLAGUE

> People don't realize that everything over which the conquest of our discourse extends always boils down to showing it to be a great big deception.[6]

5. Ibid., 74.
6. Lacan, *Anxiety*, 78.

Introduction

Psychoanalysis is a peculiar protest against the casual dismissal religion as an archaic anomaly that shall soon pass. It concordantly rejects the liberal dream of a politics without theology and claims instead the political is necessarily theological. The conscious rationale manifesting as justification for any religious belief or policy position can be addressed, mitigated, and suppressed altogether without altering the fundamentally ideological latticework of the unconscious. For reasons better or worse, religion will always triumph over the secular, psychoanalysis, and conscious theology alike, because religion is how we evolved to cope with anxiety before we could even blame the gods.

The earliest sources of religion in the archeological record begin many millennia before our species departed from predecessors, arising out of death rituals and shamanism. Religion is exclusive to the *homo* genus, but an eleven thousand-year-old temple in Turkey provides some of our oldest direct evidence of deity-worship. The Cro-Magnon mass graves in the Czech Republic (dated 25,000 years), the Neanderthal site at Regardou (65,000 years), and the *homo erectus* burials in northern Spain (350,000 years) suggest an emotional connection to death in species that predate modern capacities of consciousness. Red ocher pigments decorating skulls that were ritually "defleshed" (900,000 years) suggest we engaged in ritualistic acts long before we were *homo sapiens*.[7] The deceased's burial with its tools perhaps tells us a primitive conception of afterlife precedes our species as well. This excursus into archeology is worth reading as a parallel to psychoanalysis's two reasons for therapy; religion likewise has always had two—and ultimately only two—purposes: (1) the personal side of explanation for the inexplicable and (2) the primitive mode of tribal cohesion. The former gave us a sense of meaning. The latter was proto-politics. The earliest shamans gathered the small hunter-gatherer packs of perhaps twenty to thirty individuals to enact the magic ritual that constituted the earliest religious formulations.

> So-called "magical thinking"—always attributed to someone else—is not a stigma with which you can label the other . . . To be more explicit, recourse to magical thinking explains nothing. What must be explained is its efficiency.[8]

---

7. The dates and details of this discussion on prehistoric religion come from Barbara King's *Evolving God*.

8. Lacan, *Écrits*, 744.

Introduction

The shaman was the first subject-supposed-to-know, oscillating between the roles of priest and politician, prophet and charlatan. The placebo effect made the shaman's ritual effective, and our ancestors could not have survived without this desperate need to believe. Critique of religion elicits angst wherever it infringes upon either the purposes of (1) personal meaning or (2) tribal cohesion, and to psychoanalyze theology will require that we eviscerate both.

> Well then, the unconscious has been accepted, but there again we think that a lot of other things have been accepted—pre-packaged and just as they come—and the outcome is that everyone thinks they know what psychoanalysis is, apart from psychoanalysts, and that really is worrying. They are the only ones not to know.[9]

What then is psychoanalysis? Nobody seems to quite know, least of all the founders of the theory. Upon professing my interest in Sigmund Freud and Jacques Lacan, I often receive a question which is more a confrontation: has not modern psychology or neuroscience displaced psychoanalysis? But the question misunderstands what psychoanalysis aims to do. The Freudian unconscious, which has nothing to do with the unconscious before Freud,[10] is not in the least something that exists. We do not claim that the unconscious can be mapped by a brain scan as if it is nothing more than a hidden tier of synaptic connection. We claim the unconscious, the foundation of this theory, in the most explicit and direct sense does not exist but instead *insists*. It is not a thing but instead a way of discussing something *indirectly*. Psychoanalysis predicts behavioral repetition and schematizes what we see, but it does not in the slightest sense suppose its terminology should be read literally. On the other hand, its method should be followed with exactitude. Clayton Crockett puts it well when he cautions, "It is important to note that what Freud calls the unconscious is not an objectified entity but a dynamic principle of explanation that is testified to only indirectly."[11] Any theory worth listening to does precisely this: psychoanalysis flanks traditionally approved methods of critique, cutting across deadlocks by speaking indirectly against reality as such.

> What I am trying to do is let you in on something that is under way, that is in train, something that is unfinished and that will

9. Lacan, *My Teaching*, 8.

10. Ibid., 11.

11. Crockett, *Interstices of the Sublime*, 23.

probably be finished only when I am finished, if I don't have one of those annoying accidents that make you outlive yourself.[12]

Being a philosopher is being interested in what everyone else is interested in without seeming to realize it,[13] and psychoanalysis provokes a particular intrigue in this pursuit. In a tour for his *Écrits*, Lacan joked, "[Psychoanalysts] do not say that they know in so many words, but they imply that they do. 'We know a bit about it, but let's keep quiet about that. Let's keep it between ourselves' . . . And so we remain silent with those who do know and with those who don't know, because those who don't know can't know."[14] Later in the speech, he remarked that psychoanalysis "is not at all within the field of what we can call the coherent, but, after all, we know a lot of things in the world that survive on that basis . . . it is not for nothing that I have described it as 'propaganda.'"[15]

In *Interstices of the Sublime*, Crockett situates psychoanalysis as a method of unsettling both theology and scholarly religious theory after the death of God. Perhaps we should let the notion of *unsettling* define the goal for psychoanalytic theology. The phrase "death of God" has at least two meanings in Continental philosophy. The first is the concept of an immanent world-becoming-Spirit and Spirit emptying itself into the world, as developed in the latter chapters of G. W. F. Hegel's *Phenomenology of Spirit*. Sublimation provided the basis for Thomas Altizer's radical theology in *The Gospel of Christian Atheism*. Radical theology matured to produce several streams in the half century since. The radical theology of Altizer and evidenced in Paul Tillich emphasizes different questions from the variant of John D. Caputo and his influence in Jacques Derrida. While Caputo is generally skeptical of Lacan, Caputo's notion "God does not exist; God *insists*"[16] harmonizes with Lacan's early claim that the big Other does not exist but rather insists. Their meanings are clearly separate, for deconstruction is not psychoanalysis. But there is a theme developing where we must realize—and is this not true of religion generally?—the veracity of our beliefs have little bearing on whether or not those beliefs live on in our academies and cultures alike. Thus even in disparate streams of radical

12. Lacan, *My Teaching*, 4.

13. Lacan, *Écrits*, 671.

14. Lacan, *My Teaching*, 9.

15. Ibid., 12.

16. The notion of insistence over existence deserves far more attention than I give it here. I highly recommend Caputo's *Insistence of God*.

theology, there are points of intersection. I entered the tradition of radical theology through Caputo's introduction, and though our interests diverge, the excursion into his interests prepared me to engage the Altizerian and psychoanalytic avenues, the latter being the stream this book engages.

In turn we come to a mode of radical theology popularized by the likes of Slavoj Žižek and Clayton Crockett among so many others. The second meaning of the death of God, as Crockett explains, "can be assimilated to the linguistic turn, in which the being of God is dissolved into language non-metaphysically."[17] Lacan's claim "God is unconscious"[18] can be read at least two ways, the first evoking the image of a figure literally knocked unconscious by the incendiary critiques of materialism and the second evoking a unity between what we call God and demands of our unconscious register. The latter is clearly Lacan's primary meaning, but we should not neglect the idea of deities knocked off their pedestals; even demoted gods do not die. The claim was read poorly if the reader concludes God is nothing more than a psychic aberration of a misguided imagination. One does not understand psychoanalysis without remarking on the intersections of Jewish and Christian theology in its founding theorists.

In *The Ethics of Psychoanalysis*, Lacan claimed there could be no Sigmund Freud without Martin Luther. The death of God for psychoanalysis is not simply a claim about God's nonexistence but an acknowledgement that the question God's existence is nearly irrelevant next to the persistence and insistence of gods in our society, psyche, and language. It is the claim that the death of one manifestation of the big Other will turn out the same way it always goes when one rejects a god, namely, that we shall immediately search out a new god. It is not for nothing that Lacan famously claimed, "In the end, only theologians can be truly atheistic, namely, those who speak of God."[19] No theologian will read that line without immediately feeling a visceral truth in that hyperbolic claim. We may disabuse ourselves of tired gods, but the big Other is never threatened by our rearranged loyalties.

If psychoanalysis is concerned with what does not work, psychoanalytic theology—to place Christianity on the couch and invasively inquire of its self-sabotaging repetitions, masochism, and sadism—will be an aggressively critical theology. At times this will appear altogether cynical, but cynicism need not merely mean the politician's staged theater or the

17. Crockett, *Interstices of the Sublime*, 14.

18. See Lacan, *Four Fundamental Concepts of Psychoanalysis*, 59.

19. Lacan, *Encore*, 45.

sociopath's disinterest. Cynicism also evokes realism and negativity; these things too can be deeply good things. Sometimes society needs nothing more than a day of rage, and rage can be among the holiest of things. My wager is that the psychoanalysis of Christianity should require a healthy dose of rage deployed against the ways we (dis)engage, and those with eyes to see and ears to hear will always bring a plague.

OUTLINE OF THE BOOK

This book is organized as a theological meditation on the life's work of Jacques Lacan. The reader will doubtless already have noticed the frequent use of quotes from his seminar, public appearances, and essays, and these will continue throughout the text in order to give the reader a sense of Lacan's provocation in his own words. The book is meant to walk the reader both his general theory and specific theological themes (many of which so rarely receive attention in secondary literature). There are many topics throughout the seminar I neglect in the interests of space and relevance to theology, and though I do not always agree with Lacan, this book will read as if I do. The reader should also know that I am trained in philosophy and theology; I am not trained as a clinical psychoanalyst. I study psychoanalytic theory as a method to analyze matters of philosophy, religion, and politics. If I accomplish nothing more than convincing you to read Lacan, I will consider this effort a success. This book is partly explanation and exegesis of Lacan, but it is also my attempt to push his theory further into the practical realm of understanding religion.

To begin, Lacan was fond of quoting from his patient Picasso: "*I do not seek. I find.*"[20] At the risk of immense hubris the quote captures the power of a theory to what we often already know yet cannot find the words to convey. As Bruce Fink describes it, the goal of Lacanian psychoanalysis is to "pierce through the imaginary dimension which veils the symbolic and confront the analysand's relations to the Other head on."[21] The first chapter will explore the three Lacanian registers of Imaginary, Symbolic, and Real. Each of these are always quite different from reality *qua* reality, which brings us to a distinction between illusion and delusion. Surveys now consistently show a resurgent apocalypticism with nearly half of US Christians believing the world will end by 2050, and we need to think about what it means when

20. Lacan, *Ethics of Psychoanalysis*, 118.
21. Fink, *Clinical Introduction to Lacanian Psychoanalysis*, 35.

one of our society's most pervasive ideals is its own destruction. What is the difference between a belief attached to a wish and a belief held *against* one's wishes? The piece of reality that does not work produces the visceral reaction and intrudes upon our world as the traumatic Real that cannot be assimilated into words.[22] The Real is filtered through the Symbolic, the site of the big Other, to finally arrive at our Imaginary conception of how things are. Our paradigms always retroject onto our conscious reasoning a rationality that is not justified. Our beliefs are made for us, and we must come to terms with this if we are not to descend into psychotic delusion.

We then proceed beyond the principles governing instinct, which is fundamentally conservative in nature. The question for theology is whether it is doomed to a conserving role (which suggests religion is nothing more than a negligible adaptive feature) or contains excessive elements that propel it beyond the pleasure and reality principles. The drive is the *beyond* of the pleasure principle. In the same way that the body desires homeostasis, the psyche desires an epistemic stasis it can never quite reach. But that lack of stasis does not prohibit us from all manner of creative vicissitudes that construct an illusion of peace. The genesis of what we desire—whether an object or a belief with which we associate our identity—is always far more complex than we retroactively imagine.

There is always a difference between the *je* and the *moi*. The former is the totality of who I am—my conscious ego, my social networks and behaviors by which I navigate my world, the social norms and taboos by which I am unconsciously judged. The *moi* is the (always ephemerally) conscious perception of myself; there is a wide and awful gap between the *I* and the *me*. The unconscious is like a river; we kneel beside the river to collect a fleeting fistful of sediment and insist the river *really is like this*. But a moment later, after anxiously insisting that a token belief is essential to our identity and to reality, we cast the sediment back into the river and go on about our day. The big Other gives and takes. This process works so long as we never realize that the beliefs we have are almost entirely arbitrary and are simply representatives *in the place of* representations; the psyche has positions—Subject, Other, ego, object (cause of) desire—and the psyche maps notions onto these positions. We play along and think we have decided what was important to us, but this is always a ruse. Thus the second chapter considers the difference between theology as instinct and theology as drive in light of the *I-me* notion of subjectivity.

22. Lacan, *Four Fundamental Concepts of Psychoanalysis*, 55.

And I who stand here right now and bear witness to the idea that there is no law of the good except in evil and through evil, should I bear such witness?[23]

Abraham Joshua Heschel observed, "*Intellectual honesty* is one of the supreme goals of philosophy of religion, just as self-deception is the chief source of corruption in religious thinking, more deadly than error. Hypocrisy rather than heresy is the cause of spiritual decay."[24] As we said, Lacan was fond of the idea of a certain cultural paternity between the Protestant reformation and the discovery of the unconscious. Saint Paul and Martin Luther leveled weapons against the Symbolic Law which creates sin. In the same way, a very Lutheran psychoanalysis claims the *Thing* we desire, like sin, is desired when the Law says we cannot have it. The antagonism generates endlessly frantic activity as we seek the reacquisition of a *Thing*, which was never owned in the first place and cannot exist. Out of the regulatory superego injunctions comes what Žižek calls an "obscene excess-supplement," which is to say that every instance of Law contains a contradictory injunction to do the opposite. The third chapter explores a paradoxical theology of the Symbolic and argues that a truly Christian ethic requires us to, as Saint Paul insisted long ago and as we have ever since only ignored, confront the Symbolic head on.

> The analyst is a symbolic person as such, and he is sought out insofar as he is both a symbol of omnipotence and is already an authority or master. Seeking him out, the patient adopts a certain stance which is approximately as follows: "You're the one who possesses my truth."[25]

The fourth chapter will present the most complex material as we explore psychopathology, and I present it at the midpoint of the book in order to provide a basis for social patterns in the following chapters. The relationship of the conscious to the unconscious delivers us to our psychopathological disposition toward the Symbolic. Like Job—a quintessential illustration of an Imaginary demanding the Symbolic give account for the Real collapse of his life and which can only reorient at the moment the big Other refuses to give account—we recover from obscene narratives at the moment we realize that the big Other does not exist. This is not a simplistic,

---

23. Lacan, *Ethics of Psychoanalysis*, 190.

24. Heschel, *God In Search of Man*, 10–11.

25. Lacan, *On the Names-of-the-Father*, 35.

Introduction

metaphysical rejection but rather a materialist protest against theologies that do not work. The relationship between the conscious and unconscious delivers each of us into the hands of psychosis, neurosis, or perversion. And just as a group of quiet and amiable personalities can aggregately produce a most vituperative hostility, so to a group of normally-adjusted neurotics produce a social psychopathology of perverse cynicism. The fifth chapter explore the relationship between individual and social psychopathologies begun by Lacan that permeate the work of Slavoj Žižek. I wager the patterns of politico-psychopathology manifest as well as religio-psychopathologies. We see this with Luther, and we continue to see this today. The aggregate disposition will always conflict with the individual, and we will see individuals adopting the foreign language of a theological ideology producing anxieties that they should not have.

Through crossing Lacanian political theory with what we are currently seeing in American Christianity, we expose a series of trends within the resurgent fundamentalism of recent years. Perhaps *resurgent* is the wrong word if these tendencies were always latently present, but there is a definite sense in which long-silenced views are now putting themselves proudly out in the open. Why is this happening now, and what interests are served by the resurgence? The sixth chapter examines the four discourses (university, master, hysteric, and analyst) undergirding the analysis of communal psychopathology. We will examine Lacan's expansion of Hegel's master-slave dialect, and we will explore the concept of political theology emerging in the twentieth century through the work of Walter Benjamin and Carl Schmitt that continues today, most popularly with Žižek. To diagnose a disease requires us to know where to look so as to avoid diagnosing a mere symptom. The critique of Christianity must learn to properly diagnose the agent, the work, the production, and the truth. The hegemonic master will always beg us to misdiagnose. A choice is put to us between an irrelevant and impotent university discourse or a perceptively incisive analyst's discourse. Through crossing political theologies and the four discourses, we need to think about (1) what our theologies are producing and (2) the truth revealed by that production. This will be the most inflammatory chapter but also the most practical, as we will face as series of questions about the decline of American religion, the rise of the "nones," and the co-option of Christianity by concealed interests.

> Its truth is in motion, deceptive, and slippery. Are you unable
> to understand that this is true because analytic praxis must

move forward toward a conquest of the truth along the path of deception?[26]

Lacan is treated as either an uncannily perceptive theorist or a loathsome charlatan, and to be honest I have never quite made up my mind. Clearly his ideas have shaped me (personally as well as theoretically), but perhaps the question of theorist or charlatan *should* be somewhat irresolvable. To say something worth hearing is to say something very much outside normal boundaries, but his ideas continue to work on me. In the tenth chapter of Revelation, an angel descended and commanded the exile to eat a book that tasted like honey but made the stomach bitter. Likewise the message the angel had for kings and empire would appear alluring but result in plague. Christianity was a bitter plague upon the empire until its absorption into imperial ideology. Today the angel's message is no longer bitter, and my wager is that if Christianity desires a prophetically incisive role beyond the mere servitude of concealed interests, we should bring the Freudian plague against Christianity first. We need to think about the directions we are headed. The concluding chapter is a speculative question of charlatanism or prophecy, and likewise the unresolvable ambiguity between the two can only be dealt with the moment we consume the book.

> That [Christianity] is the true religion, as it claims, is not an excessive claim . . . when the true is examined closely, it's the worst that can be said about it. Once one enters into the register of the true, one can no longer exit it.[27]

As I said, this book is a theological meditation on the life's work of Jacques Lacan. It does not attempt a constructive theology or even attempt to answer many questions at all. Instead, as any analyst worth listening to should do, it attempts to speak indirectly against postulation at its synchronic origin. We should aim to expose the myopic conditions upon which our condemned paradigmatic notions are built. Lacan's method has ever been criticized as too opaque to make sense of and intentionally abstruse to negate the possibility of a position. *Does he ever truly mean what he says?* Perhaps it is a matter of preference. What makes Lacan interesting to me is the resistance to being pinned down, his avoidance of precise definition that somehow works on me and becomes coherent as a whole. The burdensome difficulty of his teaching, both in his day and ours, lead to

26. Ibid., 90.
27. Lacan, *Encore*, 107–8.

charges of "intellectualism," as if the hearer's inability to understand should stand as grounds to ignore. But of course, Lacan countered, "This [charge of 'intellectualism'] carries no weight, when one wants to know who's right."[28] Commentary on Lacan can only go the way of (1) reducing and clarifying beyond anything he would condone or (2) provoking ever more obscure interpretations of an already unreadably abstruse figure. I will admittedly do both. I leave much of his opacity in place to work on the reader just as it has worked on me, and though I intend this to be a close and faithful reading, I am less interested in the figure himself and more interested in using the theory to take an idea somewhere. I believe that is the only reason Lacan taught in the first place, to take analysis somewhere and put an idea to work.

> A short-lived flash of truth has come from psychoanalysis—it won't necessarily last.[29]

Freud lamented, "As a rule, the repression is only temporarily removed and is promptly reinstated."[30] We heal and then become unhealthy again, often because we allow in a voice that did not deserve to speak. The substitute satisfaction from saboteur repetitions ensure we resist our epiphanies. But the Freudian joke, like the Christian parable or the Jewish *midrash*, short-circuits the defense mechanisms that resist, triggering a truth lurking just beyond the conscious grasp. We realize we knew something all along yet resisted. So if the psychoanalysis of Christianity will require a healthy does of rage, it will also require a cryptic sense of irony. A psychoanalytic theology ends with the triumph of religion, but it begins with this: the Real is always exactly in its place; gods will always be where they have always been.

> Such is the signifier's answer, beyond all significations: "You believe you are taking action when I am the one making you stir at the bidding of the bonds with which I weave your desires. Thus do the latter grow in strength and multiply in objects, bringing you back to the fragmentation of your rent childhood. That will be your feast until the return of the stone guest whom I shall be for you since you call me forth."[31]

28. Lacan, *Television*, 13.
29. Lacan, *Triumph of Religion*, 67.
30. Freud, "Repression," 572.
31. Lacan, *Écrits*, 29.

Chapter 1

Imaginary, Symbolic, and Real

The voice of intellect is a soft one, but it does not rest until it has gained a hearing.[1]

The master breaks the silence with anything—with a sarcastic remark, with a kick-start.[2]

A s Zarathustra told us, "Many sick people have always been among the poetizers and God-cravers; furiously they hate the lover of knowledge and that youngest among the virtues, which is called 'honesty.'"[3] There is an old American anecdote wherein two rising businessmen amassed a small fortune and turned their sights on proper entry into the upper echelons of society. They possessed the funds but had yet to play the part of bourgeois elite, so to begin their climb they commissioned a famous artist to paint their portraits. The businessmen sent invitations and hosted an evening party for the unveiling. The most celebrated art critic in the city attended, and gazing upon the two portraits of the businessmen side by side on the wall with only a small, empty space between the two, the critic shook his head. Disgusted that such an obvious figure was neglected from the scene, the critic quietly asked, "But where's the Savior?"[4]

1. Freud, *Future of an Illusion*, 93.
2. Lacan, *Freud's Papers on Technique*, 1.
3. Nietzsche, "Thus Spoke Zarathustra," 145.
4. Freud, *Jokes and Their Relation to the Unconscious*, 74.

It depends on an indirect representation. By asking why Christ was not hung in the middle, he called the two businessmen thieves. The anecdote comes to us in Freud's *Jokes and Their Relation to the Unconscious*, a book exploring the way an unconscious or barely preconscious idea is triggered into consciousness. The point to maintain is brevity: "A joke says what it has to say, not always in few words, but in *too* few words—that is, in words that are insufficient by strict logic or by common modes of thought and speech. It may even actually say what it has to say by not saying it."[5] The techniques of psychoanalysis require a similar brevity. The analyst who says too much is an analyst that at once does not listen and, worse, shoves the analysand (patient) down paths she is not yet ready to traverse. The analyst is needed because she can ask better questions than the analysand is able, and good questions always contain an element of indirect representation. Epiphanies do not arise through direct regurgitation of what came before; epiphanies are unexpected slips into novelty. Surely all humanities theory, and theology in particular, is a mode of indirect representation if it has anything to say (which is not always the case).

The question of Symbolic relations and their supports in illusion is whether there can or cannot be a form of consciousness that is not deceiving itself. This chapter explores the basic schema of Lacanian registers—the Imaginary, the Symbolic, and the Real—and we will see that the analysis of a problem within one register can leave the other two untouched. We often disabuse ourselves of certain beliefs within one register and leave the problem unscathed in the Real, and this problem is easy enough to see in parochially populist forms of religion. Power abhors a vacuum.[6] Michael Hardt and Antonio Negri take this as axiomatic in their description of empire. But they also show the same problem exists within theoretical discourses where past societal relations are taken for granted and problems are critiqued that literally no longer exist: "what if these theorists are so intent on combating the remnants of a past form of domination that they fail to recognize the new form that is looming over them in the present?"[7] Put differently the three Lacanian registers suggest that for every good question there will be no fewer than three correct answers, each of which should challenge the grounds upon which the question needed to be asked.

5. Ibid., 13.

6. Hardt and Negri, *Empire*, 13.

7. Ibid., 138.

ILLUSION AND DELUSION, APOCALYPTICISM AND FUNDAMENTALISM

The subject hallucinates his world.[8]

We should begin with Freud's distinction between illusion and delusion. The wish for what could be gives rise to the *illusion*. Whether or not theology is *delusion* depends on its language means to get at. There are theologians who say what they mean, and there are theologians who say *at* what they mean; one is not necessarily better than the other, but I aim to be the latter.[9] Our ideals may be the inspiration of the divine or the flowers on the chains of our oppression, the hope that the world could be repaired or the abandonment of a world destined for wrath, necessary or irrelevant. Theology *gets at* something, but we have no guarantee that what it gets at is anything more than our need to believe in an Other ensuring security. What is certain is that our ideas are everywhere and always a form of false consciousness, a retrojected justification for what cannot quite be put into words.

Of all the ideals a culture contains which prop up cooperation in the face of our frustrations, prohibitions, and privations, Freud adamantly claimed religion has always been the chief of all ideals. A culture's ideals and values are a network of reference points for its identity, and religion, even within our fragmented and pluralistic society, provides a guarantee in the background of this network. In a qualified version of parsimony, we maintain the most oppressive and masochistic beliefs so long as they provide more security than eliminating them would. We may say we believe because our ancestors believed, because we possess proofs handed down from antiquity, or because it is forbidden to raise questions, but of course, as Freud quickly pointed out, "Such a prohibition can surely have only one motive: that society knows very well the uncertain basis of the claim it makes for its religious doctrines."[10] The motive always tells us something about the mode of operation, and prohibitions on doubt shred credibility.[11] We can think of mythic elements first as illusion, second as delusion: "Illu-

8. Lacan, *On the Names-of-the-Father*, 9.

9. I must thank Tripp Fuller for delineating these two types of theologians. It was an offhand remark in response to my frustration as I learned to read theology early in my studies. Fuller's response has stayed with me ever since.

10. Freud, *Future of an Illusion*, 46.

11. Ibid., 48.

sions [are] fulfillments of the oldest, strongest and most insistent wishes of mankind; the secret of their strength is the strength of these wishes,"[12] but on the other hand, "In the delusion we emphasize as essential the conflict with reality; the illusion need not be necessarily false, that is to say, unrealizable or incompatible with reality."[13]

While illusion is an idea founded on a wish, a delusion is an idea that is objectively false. When Columbus believed he discovered a path to the east instead of a wholly new world, it was both illusion and delusion. But what are we to make, Freud asks, of the belief that a messiah will come to heal the world? The belief is illusion, for it is doubtlessly founded on a wish, but a perpetually postponed eschatology evades the falsifiable status needed to classify as delusion. Beliefs backed by a wish deserved heightened scrutiny. On the other hand, delusions should be aggressively routed.

> Intuition is prompt, but we should be all the more suspicious of something obvious when it has become a received idea.[14]

Illusion begins when we think we understand.[15] The paradox of the illusion is that we feel illusion-complexes can be simply disabused of misinformation. Lacan emphasized the need for illusions in a strikingly different manner from Freud. The temptation for the analyst is to imagine she understands too much, because she desires to understand and empathize with her analysand. But this must be resisted, for to understand too much is to enter the analysand's fiction. He introduced this idea in the seminar on psychosis to say that what is understandable is not what is really important. One cannot understand the illusions and delusions of psychosis, for they are by definition proscribed from coherence. The analyst must always keep a distance from the justifications expressed by the analysand and not be drawn into contrived justification. There is a basic triad of frustration, aggressiveness, and regression underneath the conversation between the analyst and the analysand, and while the analyst's silence is frustrating, far more frustration would be elicited if the analyst engaged the analysand's empty speech.[16] The expression of a belief tells us something is going on

---

12. Ibid., 52.
13. Ibid., 54.
14. Lacan, *Écrits*, 207.
15. Lacan, *Psychoses*, 21.
16. Lacan, *Écrits*, 207.

underneath, but if one thing is certain it is that what truly matters is not what gets said.

> It's always at the point where they have understood, where they have rushed in to fill the case in with understanding, that they have missed the interpretation that it's appropriate to make or not to make. This is generally naïvely expressed in the expression—*This is what the subject meant.* How do you know? What is certain is that he didn't say it.[17]

Let us return to Freud's eschatological question on delusion. Apocalypticism provides a vivid example of the illusion-delusion distinction with severe ramifications for climate degradation and geo-politics. Nearly half of American Christians believe Christ will return and inaugurate the end of the world by 2050.[18] That this belief has risen during the Great Recession suggests a curiously inverted form of security connected to apocalypticism. As Žižek often remarks, it is easier for Hollywood filmmakers to imagine the end of the world than to imagine something other than our current political and economic order. What is the motivation when one of a society's highest and most commonly shared ideals entails its own absolute, unequivocal, and unavoidable destruction?

As a theologian, one cannot help but be fascinated by Christianity's desire to annihilate the world. The closely associated and pervasive belief in a rapture emerged within a period of industrial change in the nineteenth century, but this seemingly forgettable and speculative idea cemented itself into the American imagination. The rapture was a purely egoist appeal, perhaps the most genuinely American ideal (not only will the heavens reward our righteousness, but we may not even die to acquire the reward). The doctrine itself was entirely the imagination of the Plymouth Brethren minister John Nelson Darby in Ireland. Though he did not go public with his idea until some years later, Darby claimed to have discovered the rapture as early as 1827. The theology floundered in its native United Kingdom, and though Darby's acolytes devoted time and energy to spread his teachings in America, the idea appeared to be on its deathbed until 1909. In that year, the highly popular *Scofield Reference Bible* (Scofield being convinced of Darby's predictions) literally wrote the rapture into the Bible as a footnote to 1 Thessalonians, exposing most Americans for the first time to an view of immanent apocalypse that now seems as old as the New Testament it was

17. Lacan, *Psychoses*, 22.

18. Pew Research Center, "Public Sees a Future Full of Promise and Peril," 4.

footnoted in. The period is unique for the rise of American fundamentalism, the Azusa Street Revival, the subsequent rise of charismatic movements, and the increase of American missionary activity to spread *zeitgeist*
theology.

Notably, Darwinism saw its rise in this period as well but did not
become such a litmus test for populist orthodoxy until after the fundamentalist movement began to burn itself out in the 1920s and shift into
a more amiable Evangelicalism. The new apocalypticism came at just the
right moment to be inscribed as a new orthodoxy in a time and location
primed to spread its unwittingly novel and populist ideology. Apocalyptic
belief might be harmless if not for its effects on war and energy policy, all of
which must now be negotiated under the premise that even if the climate is
collapsing, are not responsible actions a futile effort against wishes of God?

What then is fundamentalism, and what is its broader connection
to our schema of illusion and delusion? It is an ethos with a particular illusion, and its staying power ensures no rise of secularism will write its
obituary. Ernest R. Sandeen joked, "Ever since its rise to notoriety in the
1920s, scholars have predicted the imminent demise of the movement.
The Fundamentalists, to return the favor, have predicted the speedy end
of the world. Neither prophecy has so far been fulfilled."[19] The five fundamental beliefs defining the American Christian variety (biblical inerrancy,
substitutionary atonement, virgin birth, second coming, and resurrection
or miracles) were clearly reactionary pillars for social controversies of the
times. The ironic analogues to today's resurgent Religious Right should not
be lost on us; Americans were told to believe these things largely through
the media investments of a small cadre of businessmen with funds to spare,
notably the two Californian oil tycoon brothers Milton and Lyman Stewart.
But these fundamentals only represented a sign of the times; had the movement formed today, the essentials would change. The ethos is the essential
and the particular beliefs accidental.

Fundamentalist movements are a specific species of delusion linked,
as Hardt and Negri have said, "by their being understood both from within
and outside as anti-modernist movements, resurgences of primordial
identities and values; they are conceived as a kind of historical backflow, a
de-modernization"[20] De-modernization invokes the misnomer character-
ized with the concept of conservatism, that is, nothing is being culturally

19. Sandeen, *Roots of Fundamentalism*, ix.
20. Hardt and Negri, *Empire*, 146.

conserved but instead constructed anew and retrojected into mythic past. "The 'return to the traditional family' of the Christian fundamentalists is not backward-looking at all, but rather a new invention that is part of a political project against the contemporary social order."[21] Protestantism's counterpart in radicalized Islam exhibits the same ethos of illusion, claiming the authority of the past in order to justify particular reactions against contemporary social order.[22] An illusion is a wish, a hope, and illusions (even delusions) can be the providence that sustains us in our trauma and anxiety. But illusions and delusions can also bring about our darkest moments.

Perhaps we should push further than Freud's assumption that religious belief is always founded on the wish. My experience is that while this is generally true, there are peculiar beliefs with culturally entrenched staying power that are held *against* the wishes of the believer. It is not uncommon for one to say in so many words, "I wish this were not true, but nevertheless this is what I am told I must believe." At times this is said to protect the believer's conscious ego from realizing she does in fact wish for the troubling conclusions of an archaic belief, e.g., in the case where a minority should be deprived of rights. But it is also very often the case that the believer genuinely wishes to believe the opposite and looks for an external Other to validate the negation of that belief. In short, it is not the delusions in general that become so difficult to disabuse oneself of; it is the counterfactual delusion sustained by a wish that remains in power in the face of all evidence to the contrary. Disabusing people of what they feel they *have* to believe but which they wish was not demanded—this turns out to be remarkably easy.

> You have to defend the religious illusion with all your might; if it were discredited—and to be sure it is sufficiently menaced—then your world would collapse, there would be nothing left for you but to despair of everything, of culture and of the future of mankind. From this bondage I am, we are, free.[23]

21. Ibid., 148.
22. Ibid., 149.
23. Freud, *Future of an Illusion*, 95.

THE IMAGINARY INVERSION

How then do we understand illusion and delusion across the conscious and unconscious registers? The Imaginary, the Symbolic, and the Real can be impenetrably difficult concepts in Lacan's work. This is largely intentional, for the three operate in a diachronic and synchronic fashion, that is to say, they cannot be entirely separated. Freudian theory cannot be grasped, Lacan claims, without knowledge of these three operations and the separate analysis of each. To analyze without them will have us mistaking the scaffolding for the building.[24] To be clear, the three registers are not things *qua* regions of the psyche, and they are not meant to be understood with exactitude. Lacan's theory is always meant to be turned over and played with as a useful tool. He avoids exacting definitions with the intent to provoke something in the student. Imaginary, Symbolic, and Real are foci for exposing patterns of behavior seen in therapy. He describes them as fields out of which ego, superego, and id emerge. The Imaginary is the tier we are most familiar with: anything conscious is Imaginary.

> When you see a rainbow, you're seeing something completely subjective. You see it at a certain distance as if stitched on to the landscape. It isn't there . . . So, what is it? We no longer have a clear idea, do we, which is the subjective, which is the objective. Or isn't it rather that we have acquired the habit of placing a too hastily drawn distinction between the objective and the subjective in our little thought-tank?[25]

An image we see is always a virtual image, a representation that is not quite reality as such, precisely because vision is mediated. The Imaginary fuses with reality *qua* reality in perception, and the very existence of optical illusions hints at the need for separating out the registers of perception.[26] The Imaginary is what is artificially produced.[27] The physics of light refraction present photons further mediated by our position and distance, the reception of the image into the occipital cortex, and the image's interpretation based on what I expect to see; all of these factors collude to make sight

24. Lacan, *Freud's Papers on Technique*, 76.
25. Ibid., 77.
26. Ibid., 76.
27. Lacan, *On the Names-of-the-Father*, 52.

possible. Experiential knowledge is always mediated. We can examine this with Lacan's bouquet illusion.[28]

Suppose we place an empty vase on top of a stand and a bouquet of flowers on the underside of the stand, with the bouquet on the underside blocked from our view. This stand is placed between ourselves and a concave mirror reflecting and inverting the upside-down bouquet. There is a precise position at which we could stand where the existing (empty) vase on top of the stand will appear to be filled with an (reflected, inverted) imaginary bouquet underneath. In this example, the mirror functions as the occipital cortex, projecting certain expected versions of the external world to my conscious experience. The vase is empty, but it looks just as it would if it were full. The further we are from the bouquet, the more parallax completes a very believable picture. This is what is meant by the Imaginary, which is not to reduce the image to something necessarily untrue. To call a concept Imaginary brackets the question of truth in favor of focusing on the conditional experience. Our temptation is always to conflate the Imaginary idea with reality as such, so introducing a series of registers into conceptual analysis allows us to describe an idea as sufficiently true in one register even if it is devoid of operative content within another register. Introducing registers allows us to separate out parts of a notion, and this confronts us with the always deceptive consciousness conditioned by elements within another register.

The Imaginary is the domain of narcissism, or more exactly, the Imaginary manifests our vocalized justifications for unconscious narcissism. Whenever we undergo cathexis (investing an object with significance) the object becomes integrated as a reference point for the psyche. Cathexis is classified as either object-libido or ego-libido, and the disinvestment of object-libido withdraws investment from the object and relocates it to the subject's psyche. We put energy into ideas, and those notions become part of us. The disinvestment and redirection process produces narcissistic fixation, as the subject becomes attached to a notion now tightly integrated into her own psyche.

> We see, then, that the differentiation of the superego from the ego
> is no matter of chance; it represents the most important character-
> istics of the development both of the individual and of the species;

28. The example of the inverted bouquet can be found throughout the seminars, beginning with Lacan, *Freud's Papers on Technique*, 78. Lacan develops a more complex schema of the inverted bouquet in the tenth seminar, *Anxiety*.

indeed, by giving permanent expression to the influence of the parents it perpetuates the existence of the factors to which it owes its origin.[29]

We could expand this Imaginary aspect with the dialectic of ideal-ego and ego-ideal. Ideal-ego (literally, an ideal me) refers to what the ego desires to become, which it will fall short of while grafting elements of that ideal into the unconscious. The term's reversal, the ego-ideal, is synonymous with superego and is therefore unconscious. What begins as the ideal-ego becomes the ego-ideal. According to Freud, the superego is both an expression of the id's object-choice and a rebellion *against* its object-choices.[30] The superego is always being molded and restructured, but modification of the unconscious always begins with an inlet at the Imaginary register. We perceive some ideal-ego, an ideal version of ourselves that we wish to become more like, and we begin to inculcate this vision into our psyche. We adopt beliefs or behavioral patters that fit that ideal, and repetition integrates some part of that ideal into our superego. We are never quite our ideal selves, but we are judged by parts of that ideal self at the unconscious ego-ideal register. In this way, conscious fixation remains in a perpetual state of flux and reciprocal influence with unconscious fixation.

> It is easy to show that the ego-ideal answers to everything that is expected of the higher nature of man. As a substitute for a longing for the father, it contains the germ from which all religions have evolved. The self-judgment which declares that the ego falls short of its ideal produces the religious sense of humility to which the believer appeals in his longings.[31]

Narcissism becomes more complex once we look at a development in Freud's elaboration. What remains the same between the two theories is narcissism as a product of cathexis, but there is a switch between emphasis from the narcissistic object to the later emphasis on the ego. At a primary level, the ego and id are left unseparated, but as Lee Edelman explains, a secondary phase of narcissism, "makes an idol of the ego, but only by means of an Imaginary identification of the ego with the Other, an identification that secures the fixity and coherence of the ego's form while

---

29. Freud, "Ego and the Id," 642.

30. Ibid., 641.

31. Ibid., 643.

activating aggressive energies to defend the integrity thus attained."[32] In the same way that one might look in a mirror and see an image more attractive than the image actually reflected, narcissism is unsatisfied with the conscious recognition of itself and compensates by creating a narrative beyond the recognition, an Imaginary beyond the Imaginary. Whether in terms of religion, politics, or grandiose self-image, it should be clear that any system promoting an individual as a representative of the big Other will run the risk of rewarding or exacerbating latent narcissistic proclivities. As Edelman writes, "*Narcissism is always a narcissism of the Other.*"[33]

The terminology quickly becomes abstruse, so let us pause with an example. Suppose we examine the motivations of a hobbyist. We should delineate the object of the drive from the object being collected as a hobby; a single object can fill two roles that are not even remotely the same thing. Lacan once entered the home of friend and found a collection of match boxes, each of which had their drawers pulled out slightly and inserted into the next box so that a ribbon was made to stretch over the mantle and across the walls of the room. While Lacan found the decor aesthetically pleasing, he was left with the impression the boxes had some *je ne sais qua* aspect for the collector.[34] The most meaningless of objects become invested with something else. A match box is, of course, something that exists in reality, but this tells us nothing of its meaning appearing solely for the collector.

> On the contrary, it is often what appears to be harmonious and comprehensible which harbors some opacity. And inversely it is in the antinomy, in the gap, in the difficulty, that we happen upon opportunities for transparency.[35]

We have all had the experience of realizing an idea has far more significance for the other person in the conversation than it has for us. What we may say as a slight against an idea clearly gets heard as an attack against the person for whom the notion became an identity marker. This is the basic example of narcissistic-fixation, though the narcissist's defense of the narcissistic object will feel like nothing more nefarious than basic integrity. There is the object, and then there is "the revelation of the Thing beyond the

32. Edelman, *No Future*, 51.
33. Ibid.
34. Lacan, *Ethics of Psychoanalysis*, 113–14.
35. Lacan, *Freud's Papers on Technique*, 108.

object."[36] We will explore the notion of the Freudian Thing later, but suffice it to say that object-fixation always exposes more than the ego realizes. If an idea is defended aggressively, it betrays an unconscious object-fixation that has nothing to do with the notion itself. Contradicting an idea that has become integrated into a subject's narcissistic complex triggers the fight or flight response and shuts down rational processes. An idea never lives on its own; it hides among others.[37]

THE SYMBOLIC, THE WOLF, AND THE GALLOWS

Man thus speaks, but it is because the symbol has made him man.[38]

If the Imaginary is the register of the conscious, the Symbolic is a register of the unconscious. The Symbolic is everything collected into our psyche from our experiences. It is from our parents and friendships, our social norms and taboos, our gods and our demons. The Symbolic is an intermediate register of sorts, the filter through which the Real enters and becomes interpreted for the Imaginary. The Symbolic is a presence expressed in absence.[39] The superego, the big Other, and the drive are Symbolic functions.

> Founding speech, which envelops the subject, is everything that has constituted him, his parents, his neighbors, the whole structure of the community, and not only constituted him as symbol, but constituted him in his being.[40]

The Symbolic is a stitch-work of trauma, ideals, and experiences that we continually absorb into our unconscious. Unconscious is a difficult term to pin down. To use an example from Lacan on coloration, negation does not function here in the same way that *un*black negates black.[41] There is of course no unconscious cortex within the brain. When we say unconscious desire, we denote what *happens* rather than the Imaginary *justification for* what happens. In the same way we can talk about a society's unconscious workings and ideological engines without recourse to

36. Lacan, *Ethics of Psychoanalysis*, 114.
37. Lacan, *Freud's Papers on Technique*, 137.
38. Lacan, *Écrits*, 229.
39. Lacan, *Ego in Freud's Theory*, 38.
40. Ibid., 20.
41. Lacan, *Écrits*, 704.

the Imaginary justifications and explanations for how society operates, we analyze the individual's unconscious with the full knowledge that no such thing exists. The unconscious does not exist; the unconscious *insists*.[42] It is quite appropriate, for example, for the statistician to discuss pervasive racist, patriarchal, or heterosexist views even though nobody ever consciously perceives themselves as bigoted. The introduction of the unconscious into cultural studies is what allows us to justify a claim about actual beliefs underlying and supporting the contrary belief one assumes herself to hold. The primary insistence of the unconscious is the compulsion to repeat. Repetition is a theme we return to repeatedly throughout this book, for it is a fundamental injunction the unconscious inflicts. Psychoanalysis focuses on the modification of the unconscious rather than the conscious, thus we should take it as axiomatic that conscious justification for a viewpoint is *always* of secondary importance.

As an early colleague of Lacan, Rosine Lefort's case study on her psychiatric patient, a child named Robert, explores the framing power of the Symbolic even within advanced neglect.[43] Robert was born in 1948 to an unknown father and a paranoiac mother whose negligence required Robert to be hospitalized for malnutrition before he was yet six months old. He was in and out of hospitalization and changed residency twenty-five times by the age of three, having been abandoned by his mother to child homes and institutionalization. He tested at an IQ of forty-three shortly before Lefort took his case at three and a half years.

Robert's behavior was highly agitated and erratic. He lacked motor coordination and had severely delayed speech development, apparently saying little more than the words "Miss" and "wolf." The first phase of treatment began after Robert's disposition toward other children went from agitated to violent. After one particularly aggressive episode wherein he attempted to strangle another child, Lefort took Robert back to his room at which point he began to repeatedly scream "Wolf! Wolf!" Sudden noises elicited similar outbursts, indicating the word's association with great fear. Lefort described him as "possessed," but she began to realize Robert's behavior was actually the inverse of aggression; he lacked any sense of possession, and his aggression toward other children was actually a form of auto-destruction. Keeping in mind Robert had no stability of residence, no connection with adults outside of institutions, and no consistent possessions, Lefort aimed

42. Lacan, *Ego in Freud's Theory*, 61.

43. Lacan, *Freud's Papers on Technique*, 91–106.

to instill in him some sense of ownership. As her strategy began to work, Lefort noticed Robert apologizing for behavior that he unconsciously experienced as aggressive. However, his obsessive-compulsive behavior continued, and his successful ritualist behavior—which Robert clearly derived some pleasure from—began to require him to scream "Wolf!" at Lefort as well.

> Misrecognition is not ignorance . . . There must surely be, behind his misrecognition, a kind of knowledge of what there is to misrecognize.[44]

As treatment progressed, Lefort became for Robert an image of his bad mother, which he designated by screaming "Wolf!" at her after he began to stage her actions in such a way that he could fitfully protest as if he were disappointed in her. Robert was essentially demanding that Lefort stand in the place of his absent mother to that he could feel legitimately angry and disappointed at someone, anyone at all. He needed a concrete representative to work out his free-floating angst. At some point, after an acute surge of aggression toward Lefort (aggression which he had never been able to express against his absent mother), Robert was exorcised and "the Wolf!" disappeared. Lefort became the substitute for a symbiotic relationship to a good mother, and though his linguistic capacity remained fairly stunted, he soon retested with an IQ of 80. A number of other projection games allowed Robert to work through his aggression, which is to say that Lefort was able to modify his nearly-nonexistent Symbolic register. She had the impression Robert had "sunk under the real,"[45] but there were two words. It turned out that the "Wolf" was selected for self-punishment, because the wolf is always frightening, always the voracious antagonist in children's stories. Allowing Robert's fantasy against his mother to fully play itself out against Lefort exposed the antagonisms and allowed a break through.

The full account of Robert's abused condition is truly horrific, but the case demonstrates the effect, even within advanced degradation of capacity and lapsed development, of playing a fantasy out such that we are confronted with the endgame of our fictions. The psychoanalytic method intentionally heightens antagonism to expose contradictions. In the same way that a debate stalls into semantics when positions cannot be stated clearly, the course of analysis requires the subject to chase their ideas to conclusions,

44. Ibid., 167.
45. Ibid., 100.

exposing the subject to the fictions she inflicts upon herself. Robert knew only two signifiers, but however negative they were they were still a start. If we did not inhabit a world of symbols, Lacan concludes, there would be no mediation between the other's desire and our desire to do away with the other.[46]

The legend surrounding the final words of Charles Frederick Peace, who was sentenced to death by hanging in late nineteenth-century England, provides another example of speaking past defense mechanisms. A priest followed the procession and dispassionately read from his book of the fire awaiting with no particular interest in whether the condemned would repent. After a time, Peace defiantly silenced him and asked whether the priest really believed in his own words or whether this was all a show. At the priest's astonished affirmation of belief in hellfire, Peace retorted that he would gladly crawl over broken glass from one coast to the other just to save a single soul if he shared the priest's belief in such punishment.

> It would be very easy to prove to you that the machine is much freer than the animal. The animal is a jammed machine.[47]

The prisoner exposed the priest's hypocrisy, which of course is the hypocrisy shared by all with a similar view of hellfire, but a more interesting transaction occurred at the Symbolic register. Had the condemned man sought to argue with the priest, a battle between the Imaginary of the priest and the Imaginary of the prisoner would have stalemated, doubtless with each feeling vindicated. Instead, the prisoner aimed at the Symbolic, the unconscious life of the priest that exposed an empty illusion of piety. We do not find a direct test of strength to be an effective response to a defense mechanism.[48] Resistance is evoked by the ego and commanded by the unconscious, so to interact with its conscious manifestations in behavioral patterns already gives up ground. Lacan taught his students to wait. When we encounter resistance, we have already given up if we rush the progress. One cannot rush the child crying "Wolf!" or the priest crying "Hellfire!" No progress can be made until the subject begins to understand what has been staked on the symbol.[49] Arguing against a defense mechanism does nothing but strengthen resistance. Resistance must be addressed indirectly.

46. Ibid., 171.
47. Lacan, *Ego in Freud's Theory*, 31.
48. Lacan, *Écrits*, 314.
49. Lacan, *Freud's Papers on Technique*, 286.

METONYMY: THE UNCONSCIOUS IS A LANGUAGE

> In the unconscious, which is not so much deep as it is inaccessible
> to conscious scrutiny, it speaks.[50]

The unconscious is a language, and the unconscious is the Other's discourse. These are two axioms repeated throughout nearly every essay and every seminar Lacan wrote, so it is worth pausing to consider the meaning these axioms in relation to a distinction between metaphor and metonymy. A metaphor signifies something beyond what it says. An allegory is always a metaphor, but not every allegory, joke, or parable carries potential beyond the immediate signification evinced. Every signifier refers to another signifier, and there is no ultimate signifier to capture all signifiers.[51] Metonymy is like a dictionary. There is no word in a dictionary that can capture the meaning of any other word without itself needing definition. Another way of saying this is that notions are contained within a mutually self-referential network. All of life is like this, and there is no fixed reference point by which we can know a fundamental and unassailable element of truth that does not require further qualification. Thus the parable, by evoking something that could not be said without its gesture, is also metonymy that escapes a singularly correct interpretation.

Saussure's linguistic structure delineated (1) signifier, (2) signified, and (3) referent. When I say that I place my glass upon a table, a signifier conveys a signified idea approximating the referent in physical reality. It does not matter that at the sub-atomic level my glass is not actually touching the table due to electron repulsion. In the normal discourse, it only seems to matter that my meaning is approximately correct. Derrida's famous introduction of the undeconstructible showed the signifier's shortcomings with the example of justice and law. What Derrida aimed at in his essay *Force of Law* is strikingly similar to Lacan's metonymy, though the labels of post-structuralist and structuralist would suggest otherwise. I do not mean to say Derrida and Lacan said the same thing with deconstruction and metonymy, but there is a familial conceptual similarity and mutual influence between the two theorists.

The signifier itself is empty. Signifiers become a language, and language is a network.[52] Lacan taught that the "sentimental mass of a current of dis-

50. Lacan, *Écrits*, 364.
51. Lacan, *Encore*, 142.
52. Lacan, *Freud's Papers on Technique*, 262.

course" is nothing more reducible than "a continuum, whereas underneath is the signifier as a pure chain of discourse, a succession of words, in which nothing is isolable."[53] For Derrida, justice is a signified ideal, and laws were the signifiers by which we try to enact the referent of a just society. But every law necessarily falls short of absolute justice, and moreover the very idea of justice falsely suggests that we share the same concept of justice. So if we aim for the ideal of justice, we must always be willing to deconstruct every constitution as soon as its failings show through in their antagonism with lived life. In the same way, we must always be willing to deconstruct the metonymy of the unconscious, understanding that whatever is in us is necessarily less than the word it seeks to describe and engage. We must do this, because there is ultimately only the fleeting link between the unconscious and the external world. The link between the signifier and the signified is a quilting point, but what emerges as a result is something else.[54] The conscious is something other than the manifest sum of its unconscious parts, or as Lacan put it, "There is no genealogy between a bucket and a turbine."[55]

> Our abortive actions are actions which succeed, those of our words which come to grief are words which own up. These acts, these words reveal a truth from behind . . . truth grabs error by the scruff of the neck in the mistake.[56]

Saussure's tripartite linguistics remain essentially diachronic, whereas Lacan's triple-register functions in synchrony. The Imaginary, Symbolic, and Real are entangled in such a way that we cannot investigate one register without invoking the other two. The unconscious should be analyzed like a language. The ego speaks its opinions—and it is true that the ego has a small option of autonomy here and there—but it is the vast river of the unconscious that turns the rudder of the ego wherever it desires the ego to go. But the ego at the helm will retroject its justifications so that it will misrecognize the truth, for as Freud observed, "Where id was, ego will be."[57] Freud described the ego's relation to the unconscious as a rider unable to control a much stronger horse or a monarch hesitating to impose a veto

53. Lacan, *Psychoses*, 261.

54. Ibid., 268.

55. Lacan, *Other Side of Psychoanalysis*, 49.

56. Lacan, *Freud's Papers on Technique*, 265.

57. Lacan, *My Teaching*, 83.

on parliament.[58] Our Imaginary register falsely believes it has control, but it veers at the whims of the Symbolic's metonymy. This will not stop us from believing we direct our lives with rational intention.

REALITY AND THE REAL

By definition the Real is the most opaque concept in psychoanalysis. In early seminars, Lacan appeared at times to conflate the terms Real and reality, but as his philosophy developed the Real took on a meaning entirely separate from material reality as such. Normally the Real means only that part of the external which enters and impacts our subjective worlds. It is generally safe to exchange the word *trauma* for Real. It is whatever ruptures the stability of our lives precisely because it is so vividly good or horrifically awful that the experience cannot be immediately translated into words or assimilated into the Symbolic without inflicting damage upon and reworking the unconscious.[59] The Real is sometimes described as a deadlock, a point where definition and conception breaks down. It refers to our experience before we conceptualize what happens, thus the definition of the Real in Lacan's work is similarly evasive on precise conceptualization.

A perfect example of Lacan's obscure description of the Real is this repeated axiom: the Real is always in its place. Early Mediterranean sailors learned they could use the stars to navigate the seas. Night after night, the stars were always in their place, and around them symbolic constellation charts were constructed so that sailors could conceptualize their routes.[60] We sailed by the position of Orion because he was always in his place without regard to the arbitrary selection of the god we painted onto the sky. But every so often a new star appears and an old star dies. A supernova challenges an age-old belief that the heavens were a perfectly unchanging series of spheres fixed around the earth. The traumas irrupting into our lives are always there beneath the surface, always reconfiguring the ways we see the world, always beyond our ability to quite put into words.

> The progress of knowledge can bear no fascination with definitions.[61]

58. Freud, "Ego and the Id," 636, 656.

59. Lacan, *Four Fundamental Concepts of Psychoanalysis*, 55.

60. Lacan, *Ethics of Psychoanalysis*, 75.

61. Freud, as quoted in Lacan, *Four Fundamental Concepts of Psychoanalysis*, 163.

And is there anything more difficult than to lay down good definitions?[62]

Lacan calls the Real that which is unassimilable,[63] the impasse of formalization,[64] a knocking at the door that wakes us up before we have gathered our wits to interpret the knocking as a visitor.[65] Perhaps it will be easier to understand by considering how when the truly unforgivable is committed against us, there is in society always a pressure on the victim to reinterpret what happened. Trauma is always in the Real, always lurking beneath the scenes in the aftermath. The unforgivable is interpreted through the Symbolic—however our culture divides up responsibility and blame—and the Symbolic pressures the Imaginary's perception of the event. But we return over and over to the event in our minds, wandering through the course of details, and at each moment we are on the precipice of reinterpretation for better or (often) for worse. The Symbolic is always precarious, always unconscious, and always open to the slightest suggestion that it should impose upon the Imaginary a new framing of a traumatic event. It is the nature of the Symbolic to be in flux, and this flux allows both maturity and the worst aspects of painful regression. The soul does not cease to be written.[66] Sometimes we heal and become unhealthy again— not because we did not adequately and appropriately deal with trauma in the first instance, but—because we allow in a voice that did not deserve to speak.

The gods belong to the field of the real.[67]

Though the gods belong to the field of the Real, Lacan lamented that monotheism did away with the whole field of the gods. There was a time in human history where evil was explicable simply on the basis of the mood swing of a god, and we felt no need to explain how evil was part of some grand design if that capricious god was not the one our household worshipped. Theodicy of the gods is remarkably straightforward; theodicy under monotheism appears to be an exercise in futility. The book of Job is a clear example of this flux, an Imaginary demanding the Symbolic big

62. Lacan, *Freud's Papers on Technique*, 264.

63. Lacan, *Four Fundamental Concepts of Psychoanalysis*, 55.

64. Lacan, *Encore*, 93.

65. Lacan, *Four Fundamental Concepts of Psychoanalysis*, 56.

66. Lacan, *Encore*, 109.

67. Lacan, *Four Fundamental Concepts of Psychoanalysis*, 45.

Other give account for Real loss. Job's friends deployed the standard explanations for evil that are still with us to this day, all of which fit into three
basic categories: (1) the gods are punishing you, (2) the gods are providing
you an opportunity to learn, and (3) others have it worse, so your suffering
is negligible and you complain out of selfishness. Job's defenses began to
weaken as the story progressed, but all the while he demand God justify
the torment inflicted on an innocent man. God was silent until the end,
until it had to be said: Who is this who darkens my counsel with words
without understanding?—Brace yourself, for I will question you and you
will answer me. But Christianity "erased the whole sphere of the gods"[68]
and left a skeleton in their place, and we are now bound to graft meanings
where there can be none.

The pietist interpretation of Job always regresses to a theme of humility, presuming there is some answer to Job's question that he simply cannot
understand on account of his humanity. The problem with conceiving a
unified theme is, of course, that most books of the Tanakh descend from
multiple authors and redactors. Job is commonly thought to be at least two
stories, one brief story of prose in the opening and concluding chapters and
another of the poetic theodicy providing the bulk of the text. The setting of
the text is very old, coeval with the early Mesopotamian attempts at theodicy, but the use of Yahweh reveals the story was finalized quite late. From
this we can see multiple versions of God sparring over epochs, the early
theodicy arguing for a primitively pietist humility before the gods and a
later Yahwist addition saying something more interesting, but what? Žižek
opines, "God is neither just nor unjust, but simply impotent. What Job suddenly understood was that that *it was not him, but God himself who was in
effect on trial in Job's calamities*, and he failed the test miserably."[69]

The notion of synchrony, which again suggests we cannot entirely
parse the Imaginary from the Symbolic and Real, demands interpretation
always be provisional and established through enigma. Or in other words,
psychoanalytic interpretation cares very little about recovering the precise
meaning of the author(s) of Job. Further, psychoanalysis presumes the subjective flux of the author results in multiple meanings of which even the
author was not aware. We cannot presume, of course, that every author of
a sacred anthology desired to promote a uniform theological message, but
aside from this we understand that the authors themselves did not know

68. Lacan, *Ethics of Psychoanalysis*, 260.
69. See Žižek, "Fear of Four Words," 56.

themselves well enough to control the messages conveyed. The very notion of inspiration depends on a metonymic synchrony producing something worth saying that cannot be entirely accounted for systematically. This position justifies any number of radical (mis)readings that have more to say than strictly traditional hermeneutics produce, one example of which Žižek gives us when he continues, "Even more pointedly, I am tempted to risk a radical anachronistic reading: Job foresaw God's own future suffering— 'Today it's me, tomorrow it will be your own son, and there will be no one to intervene for *him*. What you see in me now is the prefiguration of your own Passion!'"[70]

> Let us say that a religious man leaves responsibility for the cause to God, but thereby bars his own access to truth. Thus he is led to place the cause of his desire in God's hands, and that is the true object of his sacrifice. His demand is subordinated to his presumed desire for a God who must then be seduced. The game of love starts in this way.[71]

The Real is always precisely what cannot be accounted for, and Job's God recognized this, as if to say that nobody but a deceiver should be expected to give a coherent account for the truly horrific. And likewise, the psychoanalysis of theology must learn to guard the great questions[72] but not because questions pose a threat to be defended against. The Real is rational and the rational is Real, but the Real does not fit into the inadequate words we use to convey trauma.[73] On the contrary, a psychoanalytic theology guards and encourages the great questions precisely because they pose such a fatal threat to theologies that do not work. In what could have doubled as a defense of the Real's ineffability, Heschel wrote, "The task of religious teaching is to be the midwife and bring about the birth of the question. Many religious teachers are guilty of ignoring the vital role of the question and condoning spiritual sterility . . . Without guidance, our concern for the ultimate is not thought through and what we express is premature and penultimate, a miscarriage of the spirit."[74]

70. Ibid.
71. Lacan, *Écrits*, 741.
72. I must thank Barry Taylor for this quote.
73. Lacan, *Écrits*, 532.
74. Heschel, *God In Search of Man*, 339.

PARADIGMS AND PIETY

> Truth is nothing but what knowledge can learn that it knows
> merely by putting its ignorance to work.[75]

When Thomas Kuhn explored paradigm shifts in scientific fields, he described a controversially ambiguous relation to new data. The ambiguity and ignoring of evidence was by no means the anti-intellectual dismissal of science common today in which populists accuse the scientist of covering up contradictory discoveries. His theory taught two modes of operation working within all scientific fields, a normal mode and a paradigm shifting mode. Revolutions in discourse, he wrote, "close with a total victory for one of the two opposing camps."[76] Conceptual victory rewrites the history of a discipline such that the latest in theory verges on an Orwellian understanding of its own progress.[77] Our textbooks present scientific achievement as a steady progression, which is true for the vast majority of the time but does not reflect the process by which entirely novel ideas enter the field and demand a hearing.

In normal science, there is indeed a succession of data that builds to complete out a theory. But when a new theory arises with initially equal predictive capacity, the inherently conservative nature of scientific inquiry holds fast to the previous paradigm for as long as it can. The switch to an innovative theory lacks the steadily progressive feature of normal science and often appears as arbitrary as the old regime simply dying off, with younger practitioners trained in novel theory taking the reigns. But Kuhn also recognized this format of punctuated equilibrium rarely happens within theological communities, and he suggests lack of hierarchy is to blame. The scientific community is a closed community on account of the training and expertise it requires, and it does not particularly matter whether the broader population agrees with or even understands the latest in quantum mechanics. But religion, Kuhn claims, lacks coherent progress due to being an open community where everyone can be her own esteemed theologian.[78] I agree but with a caveat: theology usually has something of a hierarchy (either formal or, in the case of independent groups, implied by its academic theologians), but the ivory tower effect of language, training,

75. Lacan, *Écrits*, 675.

76. Kuhn, *Structure of Scientific Revolutions*, 166.

77. Ibid., 167.

78. Ibid., 160–73.

and expertise ensures most communities have little concept of the ideas developing in its upper echelons. The result is a distinct split between folk religion and the theology critiquing that folk religion. One significant difference between science and theology in the matter of paradigm shift is that science can ignore popular opinion while theology is entirely irrelevant without it.

But consider how this shift happens in individuals. A paradigm is a network of identity points. We shift to a new paradigm not because the weight of increasing evidence against a current view has successfully overwhelmed the coping ability of our current paradigm—indeed, beliefs may be chipped away with no serious damage to the paradigm's structural integrity—but instead we usually shift paradigms in an instant when *one* particular belief loses operative power. We suddenly realize everything has changed, but the catch in retrospect is that we never knew that one particular idea held such importance to the integrity of the belief network.

> The trap, the hole one must not fall into, is the belief that signifieds are objects, things . . . The system of language, at whatever point you take hold of it, never results in an index finger directly indicating a point of reality; it's the whole of reality that is covered by the entire network of language.[79]

Is not the way we justify our belief like the joke, loved by Freud, of the broken kettle? Mr. A. borrowed a kettle from Mr. B., and upon receiving the kettle back Mr. B. threatened to sue Mr. A. for returning it with a hole in the bottom. Mr. A was outraged: "First, I never borrowed a kettle from B. at all; secondly, the kettle had a hole in it already when I got it from him; and thirdly, I gave him back the kettle undamaged."[80] Each of the three defenses are perfectly acceptable independently, but altogether they show the instant shift of plausibility that happens when "and" is exchanged in the place of "either/or."

Freud's fascination with jokes and their relation to the unconscious came from their ability to say too little, and in so doing, provoke the hearer's realization that she knows more than she realizes she knows. Again, the joke brings the pre-conscious into consciousness, and—as is the case when someone objects to a joke—this transition from pre-conscious to conscious instantly elicits anxiety or anger whenever the hearer is forced to realize

79. Lacan, *Psychoses*, 32.
80. Freud, *Jokes and Their Relation to the Unconscious*, 62.

that they already know something they wish they did not know. The joke, like artwork, bypasses the normal defenses we deploy against realizing we know what we do not want to know. It is curious that a piece of music sways perspective where no argument succeeds, but such is the nature of the artist's ability to disarm, again, by speaking in an indirect manner. Freud wrote, "Only jokes that have a purpose run the risk of meeting with people who do not want to listen to them."[81] It is not unlike the old observation of Diogenes, who asked what use there could possibly be for a philosopher who never offends anyone. Surely, to say nothing of import keeps one safe from reprisal, so perhaps we should exchange "joke" in the previous sentence with critical theory in general.

How should we import the observations of Kuhn on paradigms and Freud on jokes into our understanding of individual paradigmatic changes? Let us take an example from a more familiar network. If we were to graph the Internet with points representing each site and map links between sites, it would be readily apparent which clusters were the major companies. We might not be able to tell simply from the cluster size which company was represented, but it would be clear the graph would change entirely if a hub were to disappear. We could see how truly irrelevant and negligible most sites are, and if we needed to delete one site or another the choice would be rather simple. In his essay "Two Dogmas of Empiricism," W. V. O. Quine attacked the naïveté of dogmatic empiricism by describing scientific knowledge as a web stitched with points of knowledge, with experimentation impacting the boundaries of the web. Empiricism's illusion is that it would be open to new experience so long as it were verifiable, but in fact theory seems better suited to ignore new ideas and experiences if they would do irreparable harm to the whole network. Individuals and communities exhibit a need for epistemic stasis in the same way the body desires homeostasis, and we often receive more satisfaction from the stability of maintaining deplorable ideas than we would receive from rethinking. We will even defend beliefs that do not appear at first glance to matter much to the network's integrity, but resistance always suggests more is happening unconsciously. Censorship and resistance *always* suggest an internal contradiction of which the subject is likely unaware. We can imagine how chaotic the scenario would be if the deletion of one unknown website unexpectedly cascaded and collapsed a large cluster of websites, and yet this is precisely what happens when individual paradigms shift all the time. When

---

81. Ibid., 90.

the most seemingly unimportant idea is defended and critical thought intensely resisted, the subject is unconsciously resisting something.

Psychoanalysis calls this phenomenon disavowal, displacement, or repression, and entire networks of beliefs layer themselves atop what is disavowed. The displacement is always unconscious, and the conscious must keep away anything that could filter into the unconscious-anxiety complex. Disavowal is associated with perversion, and we shall return to this defense mechanism later, but I begin its discussion here in order to shift focus from accuracy to truth,[82] the latter being what happens when we put our ignorance to work.

Whether legitimate or otherwise, everything an analysand does to block an interpretation should be viewed as resistance.[83] When the analysand expresses doubt, this is a message of resistance to the analyst. The analyst might suggest a dream-element expresses an unconscious attachment, and when the analysand doubts any such interpretation could be true, the analyst knows the heightened doubt correlates closely with induced anxiety. Anxiety in this case comes from the analysand's unconscious knowledge of the truth (which has been censored), but dissonance between what is consciously and unconsciously known requires the analysand to reject the interpretation. Doubt, particularly of the aggressively denied variety, always signals dissonance in the subject.[84]

Censorship in the unconscious leads to conscious resistance. In other words, the behavior that we see is not censorship but the result of censorship. Censorship is a flaw in the Symbolic, the Law insofar as it is never fully understood.[85] We expect a person to be subject to Law, but the mere fact that we cannot grasp the full set of rules we live under or the paradoxes and contradictions of those rules shows we are perpetual law-breakers. Thus in the same way that this is true for individuals in relation to society's norms, it also holds for the individual's relation to their Symbolic register. To call someone a criminal yields an instant denial; the perpetual state of unconscious flux produces the expression of doubts, resistances against what the analysand knows to be true (as indicated by anxiety) but cannot allow herself to express as true. But just as Descartes founded certainty upon doubt,[86]

82. Lacan, *Écrits*, 13.
83. Lacan, *Ego in Freud's Theory*, 127.
84. Ibid., 126.
85. Ibid., 127.
86. Lacan, *Four Fundamental Concepts of Psychoanalysis*, 126.

Lacan claims doubt is the precipice of new thought. Seeing resistance tells us we are getting close to the pathogenic nucleus of what is being repressed.

We live in an age of unprecedented access to information, yet paranoid and harmful ideas continue to find an audience. Like scientific models that do not work, the slightest disintegration of a disavowed idea should collapse a theology that does not work. We desire to believe now as much as ever, and we are doing untold damage in the process. We shall discuss this further in the sixth chapter, but a conspiracy theory relies on exactly this structure of displaced cynicism; what matters is not whether the ideology's proponents *really believe* in the ideas they advocate, but instead what matters is that the idea *works* as a method of tribal cohesion. This is how myths always function. A myth with staying power is not a simply metaphor but also a metonymy; myth does not articulate what is actually believed to be true about the world but instead articulates *in the place of* what is actually believed.

> A fundamentalist does not believe, he knows it directly. Both liberal-skeptical cynics and fundamentalists share a basic underlying feature: the loss of the ability to believe, in the proper sense of the term. What is unthinkable for them is the groundless decision that installs all authentic beliefs, a decision that cannot be based on a chain of reasonings, on positive knowledge.[87]

As soon as there is a symbol, there is a universe behind it. It is a machine with cracks, and those imperfections produce and guide our drives. One cannot escape Symbolic, and it tells us what we should desire. Our tribal problem today is that Symbolic systems progress to the point of non-compatibility, at which point—even with the aid of mass communication—language between groups becomes irrevocably dissimilar. Communication becomes impossible.[88] There is never simply a dialogue between two, as both subjects in a debate appeal to the external validity of the big Other. Just as the therapeutic relationship involves more than two subjects discussing one of the subject's problems—are in fact two consciousnesses and two unconsciousnesses[89]—a dialogue between two is always between four. But we have all had the experience of wondering whether the other person believes what they are saying or are instead stalling as a defense of whatever

87. Žižek, *How to Read Lacan*, 116.
88. Lacan, *Ego in Freud's Theory*, 83.
89. Lacan, *Écrits*, 357.

ideology they must be defending with a particular position. Is the person a cynic or a fool? And what drives us to serve the demon?

Psychoanalysis can only unsettle theology by relinquishing its need to explain with exactitude. The analyst must eventually provide the analysand with an interpretation, but the good analyst understands that the timing and nature of the interpretation is subject to dynamics that prioritize the analysand's health over the over interpretative veracity. We will return to a discussion of "lying sincerely" or "sincere hypocrisy" in Lacan's four discourses, but let us begin that discussion here by clearly laying out the conditions upon which all therapy (or routine advice among friends) must function: sometimes it is better to conceal truth, especially when conceal-ment proceeds into the dialectic of truth. The obsessive analysand begs the analyst for an interpretation, but the analyst knows she cannot bear the truth just yet. Lacan's seminar method follows the same elusive pattern; it is truly rare for him to say anything plainly, and rarer still that a page passes without tiers of keen insights.

> How many times have I said to those under my supervision, when they say to me—I had the impression he meant this or that—that one of the things we must guard most against is to understand too much, to understand more than what is in the discourse of the subject. To interpret and to imagine one understands are not at all the same things. It is precisely the opposite. I would go as far as to say that it is on the basis of a kind of refusal of understanding that we push open the door to analytic understanding.[90]

The truth can only be said indirectly, subversively, from the peripher-ies of experiences that do not fit well into the whole. The history of ortho-doxies usually gets told as a story of right *doxa* challenged periodically by *hetero doxa*, but of course the truth is that orthodoxy is always constructed and proclaimed from the winner of the contest between two prospective heterodoxies. The right is only decided in retrospect after we have decided on the wrong. We then condemn the heterodoxy to obscurity, but it remains on the books and scholars later return to mine the insights it contained all along. It is the same with any perspective outside the hegemonic whole. Let us recall that whenever the subject of science came up, Lacan took pains to label psychoanalysis as a science on the one hand while in some vague sense questioning its scientific status in the next sentence. It is a science, and certainly a method, but psychoanalysis does not try to be a science in

90. Lacan, *Freud's Papers on Technique*, 73.

quite the way the term is usually meant. If psychoanalysis is to be a useful heterodoxy, it must challenge the idea that useful explanation and correct interpretations necessarily correlate. Crockett sees this when he aligns the problem theology must overcome with the problem psychoanalytic theory tackles, namely, "the need to attribute a proper and determinate meaning or referent to theological or psychological language that represents a reductive explanation. And the most harmful view is the obsessive need to consider a discourse to be theology or psychology only if it results in such an explanation."[91] We understand but only on the condition that we refuse a certain kind of understanding.

91. Crockett, *Interstices of the Sublime*, 50.

Chapter 2

Beyond the Pleasure Principle, Beyond the Reality Principle

Life is only caught up in the symbolic piece-meal, decomposed. The human being himself is in part outside life, he partakes of the death [drive]. Only from there can he engage in the register of life.[1]

So, what I've been conjuring up for you here isn't metaphysics. It's more of a brainwashing.[2]

ADDRESSING HAMLET'S DISMISSAL OF Horatio—there are more things in heaven and earth than are dreamt of in your philosophy—Georg Lichtenberg retorted, "But there is much, too, in philosophy that is not to be found in heaven or earth."[3] The absurd defense says something to the nature of this chapter, which will complete the basic introduction to Lacanian theory I wish to lay out before proceeding. The concepts in these opening chapters reflect more than what is found in heaven and earth, that is to say, we are discussing schemas Lacan claims will work even though, to take the obvious example, there is no such entity as a big Other stowed away in the unconscious. To repeat the incisive hubris of what Lacan saw his work to accomplish, it is not so much important that all is immediately understood; what is important is that the idea begins to work on us.

1. Lacan, *Ego in Freud's Theory*, 90.

2. Lacan, *Anxiety*, 69.

3. Freud, *Jokes and Their Relation to the Unconscious*, 72.

This chapter will ask whether theology acts as an instinct or a drive, for the difference between the two decides whether it should be set aside. We conceive of our desires and needs, our wishes and lusts, and our fears and hopes as aiming to quell a demand. But desire is always more complex, multifaceted, even arbitrarily so. Freud's innovation in *Beyond the Pleasure Principle* was precisely to say, contra age-old accepted wisdom, that human beings do not ultimately seek happiness. The observation may seem natural for us now—the very existence of psychotherapy as a lucrative profession depends on our masochism—but in the observation turns out to create possibly insurmountable problems in the fields of ethics and political economy. How are we to maximize the happiness of all if a death drive suggests our unconscious aims are quite the opposite?

QUILTING POINTS EX NIHILO

The life instincts are fundamentally conservative in nature. The pleasure principle regulates instinctual or biological needs and aims to reduce states of tension. On a long enough timeline, the tension produced by life is leveled entirely at death; all of biological life follows this pattern. The pleasure principle is homeostatic *par excellence*: when we are hungry, we satisfy the pleasure principle by consuming until satiation. Tension aims toward un-tension. It causes us to search for what we cannot attain.[4] The pleasure principle's excessive needs are tapered by the reality principle, which steps in to impose a limit on excessive seeking. The two principles dominate the conscious and pre-conscious systems, but something distinct emerges that goes beyond these principles at the level of the unconscious.[5] Whatever is *beyond* the homeostatic life instincts is the drive.[6] There is need and there is pure excess, the latter bringing with it everything destructive and creative. Religion normally sides with conservation, and if this is the case then religion is a life instinct. That religion is an evolutionary adaptation seems beyond doubt, but if it is conservative in nature, if it simply supports our

4. Lacan, *Ethics of Psychoanalysis*, 68.

5. Ibid., 48.

6. We should note a matter routinely lamented by Lacan, that being the Standard Edition's translation of *Trieb* as instinct rather than drive. Though this is a significant point for Lacan about how to translate Freud, Lacan's translators occasionally translate *Trieb* as instinct as well. I have placed drive in brackets wherever the English translator of Lacan confused the terms.

crudely animal instincts, then an adaptation is all it is. If religion should become more than an adaptation, we need to think of theology in terms of drive.

Lacan was something of a creationist, or at least he claimed as much. For better or worse, *creatio ex nihilo* produces a quilting point for meaning. Always beware evolutionism, he told his students,[7] for "I have already indicated the necessity of the moment of creation *ex nihilo* as that which gives birth to the historical dimension of the drive."[8] The doctrine *creatio ex nihilo* holds such a prominent place in psychoanalysis, because at some point signifiers enter the world and make an irrevocable change in the subject. He continues, "In the beginning was the Word, which is to say, the signifier. Without the signifier at the beginning, it is impossible for the drive to be articulated as historical."[9] God is the beyond of the Symbolic or the Thing coextensive with the creation of the Symbolic. God is what is outside the system that makes it possible to found the system. This conception of God foreshadows the famous claim he would make more than a decade later— that only a theologian can be a true atheist—but in his commentary on *creatio ex nihilo* he can only go so far as to say that his creationist perspective remains the only avenue for the materialist's elimination of the gods.[10]

Žižek finds an example of creation from nothing in Lubitsch's *Ninotchka*, wherein a man enters a cafe and orders a coffee without cream. The waiter must regretfully inform the man, "Sorry, but we have run out of cream. Can I bring you coffee without milk?"[11] The absurdity of a bad joke becomes horrific when we desire economy without recession, but all that is available is capitalism effectively without democracy. Or consider our desire for military intervention without casualties when all that is available is a drone war without end. The difference of "without x" creates a new meaning out of absence. We find another example with man who goes into a hospital terrified he has a fatal illness though suspicious that he is simply a hypochondriac. The physicians take his symptoms and tell him, "First the good news: we definitely established that you are not a hypochondriac."[12]

---

7. Lacan, *Ethics of Psychoanalysis*, 213.

8. Ibid., 213.

9. Ibid.

10. Ibid.

11. Žižek, *Žižek's Jokes*, 47.

12. Ibid., 54.

Creatio ex nihilo is part and parcel with the fundamental lack in the Symbolic order that directs the drives and desires of the analysand. To explore what theological language even is, we will explore concepts of drive, subjectivity, the Thing, and repression. We are going to have to suspend our inclination to believe in the evolution of thought for a moment to envision theology as a short circuit rather than a metaphysics. As Crockett asks, is it possible to construct a productive theology, one that short circuits narratives without producing the disavowal constitutive of orthodox theologies?[13] Let us lay out some terms out of nothing on the assumption that a struggle for meaning from a pregnant nothingness[14] is how all creative thought already works, and let us hope that the instantiation of new signifiers should give us a new avenue for critique. The alternative is orthodoxy, which, Lacan laments—and we should take this observation very seriously—is the language one holds onto when one has nothing to say of the doctrine itself.[15]

THE (DEATH) DRIVE

> As far as the object in the drive is concerned, let it be clear that it is, strictly speaking, of no importance. It is a matter of total indifference.[16]

Drive has four distinct elements—thrust, source, object, and aim—but it is the latter two that make drive so peculiar when compared to biological instinct. Unlike instinctual needs, which seek easily attainable states of un-tension, drives are set in motion and derive always-excessive enjoyment (*jouissance*) precisely by aiming at *not* being satisfied by the desired object. Need selects an object and is satiated by acquisition. Drive selects an object and aims to encircle it rather than to directly acquire it.[17] Getting what we desire has the peculiar facet of destroying its luster. Only what is elusive can be sustained as a fantasy.

A most basic psychoanalytic axiom claims the prohibition creates the desire. The drive aims to encircle its object (object *a*) and excessively

---

13. Crockett, *Interstices of the Sublime*, 80.

14. Ibid., 183.

15. Lacan, *Écrits*, 205.

16. Freud, as quoted in Lacan, *Four Fundamental Concepts of Psychoanalysis*, 168.

17. Ibid., 168.

enjoys (*jouissance*) nearly missing the object. In a sense, *jouissance* is always substitute-satisfaction; put differently, substitute-satisfaction is the only continuing satisfaction we can have. We will explore this later in dialogue with Saint Paul, Luther, and Law, but it is helpful to understand that what makes the forbidden cookie jar appealing to the child is the same thing that makes for self-destructive repetition later on. The removal of the prohibition—this is one of Christianity's innovations and why its structure is similar to psychoanalysis—destroys the attraction of the object. But in addition to being an object *of* desire, the object *a* is better conceived of as the object *cause of* desire.

Henry Krips uses the example of a suitor courting a young woman with a chaperone in tow. The presence of the chaperone, normally an older woman from the girl's family, acts against the suitor's access to his beloved. But the personified prohibition of intimacy has the side-effect of enticement: "The chaperone is covertly instrumental in producing a certain quotient of pleasure for the suitor. This arises not from the attainment of desire or even the contemplation of such attainment but rather from engaging with the chaperone, in particular from successfully allaying her suspicions and evading her scrutiny."[18] Situating this idea of drive and desire firmly in theology becomes more interesting if we identify God with the big Other, because Lacan locates drive firmly in the Symbolic. We desire what we are told to desire by the world around us, and drive is only sustained as long as the lost-object is held aloft in teleological fantasy.

> I have led you to the point of apocalypse or of revelation of something called transgression. This point of transgression has a significant relation to something that is involved in our inquiry into ethics, that is to say, the meaning of desire . . . There is no way one can reduce desire in order to make it emerge, emanate, from the dimension of need.[19]

THE BIG OTHER AND THE LACANIAN SUBJECT

Modern debates on subjectivity tend to center on dualistic body-soul perspectives against naturalistic perspectives, the latter normally denying the existence of a soul or essence apart from materiality. Naturalism may

18. Krips, *Fetish*, 23.
19. Lacan, *Ethics of Psychoanalysis*, 207.

conform more appropriately to modern neuropsychology, but psycho-analysis does not quite fit into either perspective. Instead, psychoanalysis schematizes the person as comprised of four basic positions upon which identities are mapped: Subject, Other, ego, and object.

> Why not look for the image of the ego in shrimp, under the pretext
> that both acquire a new shell after every molting?[20]

It is worth emphasizing that the object *a* is not any specific object (cause of) desire. It is never a specific identity marker. The object *a* is a position the psyche inevitably fills by mapping upon it a desired object. The real world object that fulfills the object *a* is entirely arbitrary. Whether we affiliate with this political party or that, this lover or that, this life goal or that, this theological tribe or another, there is an empty position onto which objects of desire will be mapped. We may molt our identities, affiliations, and ideas, but the basic structure survives the molting.

The Lacanian view of the subject is comprised of four features, and of those four—A (*Autre*, big Other), the subject, the *a* (ego), and the object *a* (the object or cause of desire)—the beginning is the big Other. Lacan claims with this schema that subjectivity, the totality of who we are and what we believe and do, is dominated and primarily directed by the big Other. Our subjectivity is necessarily informed by the norms we assimilate into our psyche as the big Other. Objects are selected for the ego, and then these objects of desire shape the ego's identity. Notice again that the relationship is not an ego that selects an object but instead an object that acts upon an ego. We do not choose our identities or beliefs any more than we choose with whom we fall in love; our objects choose us.

There is no clear division between the individual big Other and the big Other demonstrated by society as a whole.[21] We are a fabrication of many things, our own conscious decisions, of course, but also of a great many things outside our control. The individual big Other and the society's big Other are mutually reciprocal, but clearly the social Other has primary control when compared with the meager power of any one individual. The unconscious Symbolic is primary, the Imaginary is an afterthought.

---

20. Lacan, *Écrits*, 217.

21. This is not to say that the Lacanian big Other is in any way a Jungian collective consciousness. I only mean to designate a reciprocal relation between individual and collective, with the power clearly lying in the latter.

DAS DING IS A VASE

An earlier version of Lacan's theory used the language of the Freudian Thing (*das Ding*) instead of object *a*. The Thing is not the thing(s) we seek after but the ultimate Thing, the space that hints something is missing and needs to be re-found. The Thing is like the emptiness of a vase, an object that exists only to be filled. The vase designates an empty space which we would not have thought of as empty without it. Any bouquet will do but the selection of an arbitrary flower does nothing to remove the sense that *something* needs to fill the Thing. Our attachments wax and wane, rise and fall like a see-saw of desire as we try to discover the version of ourselves (ideal ego), but our seeking is in vain.[22] We search for the ideal self by looking for the Thing that will cover the void, but a Thing that never existed cannot be re-found.

> If the vase may be filled, it is because in the first place in its essence it is empty. And it is exactly in the same sense that speech and discourse may be full or empty.[23]

The analyst becomes the subject-supposed-to-know for the analysand, and while the analysand may continue to imagine the analyst holds a solution, the point is for the analysand to experience heightened anxiety at their problems being "found out." We know this feeling if we have ever been asked a difficult question by a friend and hesitated before we lied, hoping our friend would not notice deception. Whether or not our semblable noticed the lie is somewhat irrelevant; what matters is that we transferred the suppose-to-know status onto the friend, and fear over the truth being found out has exposed us to the anxiety-ridden hypocritical contradiction in our lives. Until this moment of transference, therapy is just a waiting game. If an analyst (if any person of authority) handles this responsibility lightly—perhaps suggesting an bad interpretation of what is happening in our lives—we can easily adopt beliefs about ourselves that will plague our unconscious without end.

The Thing and object *a* are used side by side in the seminar on anxiety, where Lacan says the object *a* is a dead end telling us we will never acquire the Thing.[24] Again, both terms are structural categories: for want of access to some ideal Thing, we map an actually-existing thing onto the

22. Lacan, *Freud's Papers on Technique*, 174.

23. Lacan, *Écrits*, 120.

24. Lacan, *Anxiety*, 271.

position object *a*. One could say we seek access to something in the Real, but settle for something in the Imaginary. Closely associated with the relationship between Thing and object *a*, the sense of the uncanny provoking anxiety. If anxiety occurs where the barrier to *jouissance* breaks down and we suddenly fear there is nothing between us and the object we desire, the uncanny is a feeling provoked by anomalies but instead where the norms regulating what is or is not an anomaly break down. As we will soon see with the discussion of the doubt, the sense of the uncanny is where anxiety starts.[25] Anxiety is where repression begins, and the need for repression is where both negative derivatives and creative sublimation become possible. Thus the Thing and the sense of uncanny (like the big Other) are not God, but they instantiate a theology.

Crockett recognizes the tendency of these terms (Other, Thing, object *a*, Symbolic) to become progressively obscure, so let us return to his delineation: "The desire for the Other establishes the symbolic order and structures conventional morality around the Good, defined as what the Other wants . . . The desire for the Thing manifests a profound desire for the Real, which cannot exist outside of the symbolic order without any reference to the Other, but it is this desire that Lacan identifies as ethical."[26] In other words, we desire an Other that can precisely demarcate what is ethical, or perhaps we desire a big Other that will chart a proper destiny for our lives and ensure our lives will have access to the Thing. That desire never quite works, demanding as it does direct access to a God unconditioned by the Symbolic.

The devout parent often deals with this anxiety when a child asks about the fate those who have never heard of Christ or whether the family would be Christian if living in non-Christian environment. We desire a God, but only a God that is not conditioned by our cultural parameters (which seems to be a rather important facet of being a God, that is, not changing at the whims of popular opinion). But if the parent were to say what is almost certainly the case—had the child been born under different conditions, she would not be raised Christian—the irony is that the child would likely feel no anxiety. Without a culturally conditioned theology, the child clearly does not yet have the sensibilities to designate systematic anomalies. It is not the child that feels anxiety but the parent. Or further, the parent feels anxiety in the third person via the child, which protects

25. Ibid., 42.
26. Crockett, *Interstices of the Sublime*, 62.

the parent from full exposure to anxiety by unconsciously using the child's (supposed) anxiety as a barrier against their own. It is the parent that wants direct access to the Thing without the mediation of the everything in the Symbolic order, which, unfortunately for the parent, makes for a good description of psychosis. Crockett continues, "The Thing is not God, but it can encapsulate the desire for God. At the same time, it can also foreclose access to God."[27]

Another way of saying this is that we desire a God we can control, and our fear—like that of the narcissist overcome with spousal jealousy—is that our God might not be where we want it to be, untouched and unconditioned in the Real. For all their differences, Jung made an interesting assertion in his autobiography that all jealousy is routed in a lack of love. Jealousy is a particular form of anxiety, and in Lacanian terms jealousy is a demand to control the Other, to mold the Other into something that it is not. But a God purely in the Real would be more like Aristotle's unmoved mover than the God with which Abraham could barter. A God purely in the Real would not be a God that Moses could persuade to change. A God purely in the Real, unsullied by the world, is a lifeless statue. So, Lacan asks, what could be the most uncanny thing to experience when staring at a statue?—to come alive and show that the thing that once had a predictable place now has desires of its own.[28] It is not for no reason that theologies questioning the untouchable sovereignty of God are so swiftly targeted by the self-proclaimed gatekeepers of orthodoxy.

TROMPE L'OEIL AND THE GAZE

> I always speak the truth. Not the whole truth, because there's no way, to say it all. Saying it all is literally impossible: words fail. Yet it's through this very impossibility that the truth holds onto the real.[29]

To say *I am lying*—a lie if true, true if a lie—demonstrates a split between the enunciator of speech and the signifier the enunciator uses to designate herself.[30] The *I* speaking is not the same as the *I* spoken of. Let us split the double *I* into two people with an old joke Lacan was quite fond

27. Ibid., 63.
28. Lacan, *Anxiety*, 271.
29. Lacan, *Television*, 3.
30. Lacan, *Four Fundamental Concepts of Psychoanalysis*, 37–38.

of: "Why are you telling me you are going to Cracow so I'll believe you are going to Lemberg, when you really are going to Cracow?"[31] The split between communicative speech and the signifiers used to carry that message often produces an opposition to explore the bi-polarity of every drive. Let us take the scopic drive as an example: we look at the world, and the world looks back at us. We gaze upon the Other, but the Other's returning Gaze reflexively constructs our identity.

> The unconscious is the chapter of my history that is marked by a blank or occupied by a lie: it is the censored chapter.[32]

Put more simply, we tend to think of ourselves as subjects interacting with external objects. This is our experience of the world: we interact with them, and they interact with us. I identify myself as x, you identify yourself as y. But the Lacanian schema inverts this naïve notion. When my ego consciously perceives the world, I think of myself as a conscious subject in full control of my faculties and decisions. I would rather ignore the profoundly simple and wholly opposite truth: every decision my ego supposedly makes is contingent upon countless other factors steering my reality. Rather than subjects interacting with objects, we are more like objects facing and interacting with acting subjects. Or further, the *me* (*moi*) is an object contained within an *I* (*je*), and the *me-I* interacts with other objects contained by other subjects. The relationship between the ego and the unconscious results in the individual and communal psychopathologies we will discuss later.

> In fantasy, the subject experiences himself as what he wants at the level of the Other . . . in the place where he is truth without consciousness and without recourse. It is here that he creates himself in the thick absence called desire.[33]

The relationship between drive and fantasy depends on slight imperfections in repetition. Let us take the example of a child demanding to hear the same story over and over.[34] The child excitedly catches the small slips in the retellings and is happy to point out the mistake to the parent. If the parent were to retell the story with such precision that no slip was made,

---

31. Lacan, *Écrits*, 436.

32. Ibid., 215.

33. Lacan, *Triumph of Religion*, 45–46.

34. See Krips, *Fetish*, 15–18. A similar point is made in Lacan, *Écrits*, 757, regarding the dog-cat game.

the child would lose interest. Repetition "demands the new,"[35] because it requires just the right threshold of variance. It is not *repetition of need(s)* but *need of repetition*,[36] the shift of wordplay suggesting our actions are disconnected from any sensible imperative when we deceive ourselves into perpetual re-engagement with old patterns.

Something similar happens with *trompe l'oeil*, an art form that only works if the viewer tricks herself into believing the picture is a window looking out on a landscape. Lacan described a passive-active component to the drive with the classic story of Zeuxis and Parrhasios. A contest was staged for the two painters, and on the day of the unveiling Zeuxis seemed to have the upper hand with his painting of a grapevine. He watched with delight as his work fooled even the birds attempting to land on the vine's branches. What could beat fooling the birds? Zeuxis turned to Parrhasios and demanded he unveil his painting. But Parrhasios had already prevailed at the moment of this demand, having painted something so lifelike that Zeuxis took it to be only a veil.[37]

The *trompe l'oeil* style requires the viewer to stand in a very specific place in order for the brain to see the picture as if it were a window. That this once-popular art form decorates countless cathedrals is perhaps telling: we derive a fleeting pleasure from tricking ourselves into a perspective (if only for a moment). In retelling a story to a child, repetition is normally harmless. In adulthood, the repetition-drive will be a cause for therapy. In art, repetition is as harmless as *trompe l'oeil*. In religion and politics, repetition becomes a deadly "staged theater"[38] of changing things just enough so that nobody notices things are basically the same. Repetition, even self-sabotaging repetition, is demanded by the big Other and it produces virtually unlimited enjoyment in the incalculable derivations of behavior we enact. Put more directly, the big Other has a death drive.

THE PRODIGAL, ANXIETY, AND DOUBT

> In the drive, there is no question of kinetic energy; it is not a question of something that will be regulated with movement . . .

35. Lacan, *Four Fundamental Concepts of Psychoanalysis*, 61.

36. Lacan, *Anxiety*, 93.

37. Lacan, *Four Fundamental Concepts of Psychoanalysis*, 103.

38. See Žižek, "Paul and the Truth Event," 85.

It has no day or night, no spring or autumn, no rise and fall. It is a constant force.[39]

The first triad we need to explore lies between frustration, aggressiveness, and regression. We find these three always linked in a perpetual flux. We have all had the experience of fearing for a friend who seems perpetually caught in a strategy of self-sabotage. The reality principle, in this case the culturally imposed realities that limit our excessive pleasure-seeking, normally steps in to regulate the pleasure principle. But the limits of what is beneficial are disregarded by our self-saboteur friend. Why? No matter how much one insists they want or need happiness, there is an excessive drive that acquires far more satisfaction from *encircling* the object of desire than it does from immediately acquiring the object.

> There are empty desires or mad desires that are based on nothing more than the fact that the thing in question has been forbidden you.[40]

The parable of the prodigal son puts on display the pleasure principle's regulation by the reality principle. After quickly squandering his inheritance, the harsh realties of financial lack force the son to return home to his wealthy father, who represents the security of the big Other. And indeed, a stable ideology provides a sense of security. But a better reading of the parable exposes the underside of the big Other's security; the big Other commands us to enjoy, but it judges us for enjoying. Kester Brewin argues the parable should be read as a tragedy wherein a young adult on the verge of ideological separation from the father—after all, maturity requires precisely this element of rebellion if the child is to become its own person—regresses to childish submission.[41] All that changed by the end of this tragic parable was that the son no longer had a future inheritance, because the big Other voiced intent to give all remaining fortunes to the brother that did not rebel. The son desired to preserve, maintain, and protect the Thing like a primordial vase, to which Lacan can only conclude, "The further he goes down this path . . . the more he is taken in."[42] The big Other threw the son into the world to find *jouissance* but promptly accepted the son back into the fold of control. All drives are ultimately death drives; they are excessive,

---

39. Lacan, *Four Fundamental Concepts of Psychoanalysis*, 165.

40. Ibid., 243.

41. Brewin, *Mutiny!*, 115–20.

42. Lacan, *Anxiety*, 41.

beyond regulation, and constantly flirt with destruction. But death drives, by breaking the normal regulation of the pleasure and reality principles, are also sources of creativity.[43]

[The big Other] is saying this to me, but what does he want?[44]

The idea of death drive, Lacan readily admits, is hyperbolic and scandalous. It is an idea that can only work on the assumption that the death drive, like the unconscious containing it, is not a thing that exists but a pattern of repetition that *insists* beyond the stable cycles of need and satisfaction.[45] We could twist the popular Christian mantra that within each person there is a god-shaped hole: it is the big Other who has a lack, and it does nothing but cause us anxiety. This is the Gaze of the big Other on full display: "What do you want?—you need only ask and it is yours!" returns with only the feeling of being watched and judged by the world. The Gaze tells us nothing and everything, and we will live our lives trying to please this Gaze.

The seminar on anxiety came in the year before the seminar on the Gaze, and one sees a continuity between the two. Contra the notion that anxiety is fear without an object, Lacan is adamant that anxiety must have an object in the Real. But because the Real is beyond words, anxiety has the effect of feeling free-floating. Anxiety is the ego's signal that something has happened in the Real (which is quite different from saying there is anything actually worth feeling anxious about in reality).[46] Anxiety is a middle space between what we desire and the enjoyment of what we desire.[47]

Anxiety sets the drive in motion. Out of the nebulous question of what we desire, anxiety has a way of plucking desire out of the ether and concretizing our options. This is how Lacan reads the Christian myth of incarnation: "God is soulless. That is quite evident, not a single theologian has ever dreamt of attributing Him with a soul. The radical change of perspective in the relation to God began, however, with a drama, a passion, in which someone made himself God's soul."[48] The object *a* is always the thing sought after as a lost or fallen object, what we desire to make

43. Lacan, *Ethics of Psychoanalysis*, 212.
44. Lacan, *Four Fundamental Concepts of Psychoanalysis*, 214.
45. Lacan, *Other Side of Psychoanalysis*, 46.
46. Lacan, *Anxiety*, 173.
47. Ibid., 178.
48. Ibid., 164.

us whole again. But on the other hand, object *a* was never lost because it never existed. The ideal of fulfillment can only be approximated, and the objects we concretely seek—whether material or ideological—do not make us whole because they cannot restore a state that never existed. In Lacan's reading of the incarnation, the soul is the object *a* that God never had, and a soulless being is nothing but anxious. When the Word became flesh and dwelt among us, the Christ figure gave God not only a body but also in some sense a soul.

Lacan could be accused of a flimsy supercessionism at this point. After all, was he saying Yahweh was an anxious obsessive who needs the Christ-analyst to set history in motion? Perhaps, but I do not think we have to take his analogy so far. As we shall see in the following chapter on ethics, psychoanalysis is far more theoretically similar to Lacan's nominal Catholicism than Freud's latent Judaism, but this is not to force a contest between the two. To remove the prohibition, as Christianity does by nullifying the Law, creates the condition of anxiety. What can be said, for better or worse in each, is that Judaism concretizes the Symbolic with the Torah whereas Christianity concretizes anxiety by nullifying the Torah.

If the death drive is the site of creativity as well as destruction, we should pause to reflect on the relationship between anxiety, repression, and creative thought. Crockett notices an inversion of the relationship between anxiety and repression in Freud's thought as it matured. Early on, Freud supposed our anxieties result from repression, which is an easy conclusion to make supposing that the lack of satisfaction implied in the state of repression produces the feeling that there is something we must be missing. As his work evolved, Freud reversed course and claimed that anxiety is primary, and repression follows as a solution. This conception of anxiety as primary is consistent with Lacan's description of anxiety as the mediator between the object we desire and access to *jouissance*. Crockett explains, "If repression precedes anxiety, it is negative, and issues a repressive theology that remains in denial and is constantly threatened by an anxiety that it cannot contain, which takes the form of a return of the repressed. If anxiety precedes repression, then theology is constructively repressive in a self-aware manner because it attends to the anxiety, writing it large in and as the body of God."[49]

Crockett argues we can better conceive of creative thought as an after-effect or derivative of repression, which in turn is a return of a primary

49. Crockett, *Interstices of the Sublime*, 95.

anxiety. Wherever there is theology, there is anxiety, and on the knife's edge of anxiety we are perpetually open to creative possibilities and at risk of regressive thought. The relation of theology is fluid and produces a back and forth experience of the negative and positive. He concludes that theology finds productive creativity through embracing its true nature, that is, repression responding to anxiety rather than anxiety as such.[50] In short, theology already is a return of the repressed.

> Why is it that people aren't happy about the world being so in order, ever since the Neolithic period—because we can't go back any further—that everything should merely amount to insignificant wavelets on the surface of this order? In other words, why do we want so much to preserve the dimension of anxiety?[51]

We now turn to the nature of doubt. If frustration, aggressiveness, and regression constituted a first triad, we now turn to a second way of exploring this as inhibition, symptom, and anxiety. Let us take it as axiomatic that "anxiety is not doubt, anxiety is the cause of doubt."[52] Anxiety is that which does not deceive; it is telling us something about a flaw in the Real. Anxiety is not something we feel when we cannot have what we want but rather an experience of a barrier removed. Anxiety is the middle ground between the object *a* and *jouissance*. Consider these two scenarios, one in which we are told we cannot have what we desire and another in which we are told our own decisions are all that stand in our way. The latter case, where the prohibition is vacated (or recognized as self-instantiated) creates far more anxiety. Is not this fear of excessive enjoyment precisely what we find in those anxiously protesting the dissolution of society's moral norms?

Let us return to the relationship between the uncanny and doubt. We can absorb even very terrible experiences without the sense that there is anything remarkably anomalous about the experience. The uncanny is specifically a feeling that something *should* be an anomaly, but we suddenly realize the norms governing what we should expect are lacking. The uncanny gives rise to anxiety, and anxiety gives rise to doubt. Thus doubt is an uncontrolled process triggered by the removal of barriers. It is not a process the ego actively chooses to engage. When we begin to dismantle our old beliefs in an organized and progressive way (that is to say, when we *choose* to doubt), we are engaging in something different than what Lacan

50. Ibid., 96.
51. Lacan, *Anxiety*, 38.
52. Ibid., 76.

43

means by doubt, which is not something within the control of our faculties. Just as beliefs choose us, they leave us without our permission. Recall the earlier discussion of illusion and delusion and my claim that dismantling counterfactual beliefs lacking a corresponding wish (that is to say, a delusion that is not an illusion) is actually remarkably easy. It is easy because the lack of a supporting wish produces a believer ready, even eager, to discard an idea once she feels authorized to breach a barrier. We respond to it with symptomatic frustration, aggression, and regression, but doubt is only the initial breach.

REPRESENTATIVE-IN-THE-PLACE-OF-REPRESENTATION

Psychoanalysis goes further than claiming there is a fundamental and constitutive lack in ourselves that we are searching to fill; it claims that filling that lack would stop all motion of the subject. Ludwig Feuerbach described theology as an exploitation of deficiencies in our knowledge that confuses the depths of nature with divinity.[53] The theist, he claims, "thus extends *the limits of his intellect to limits of Nature*,"[54] but the childlike explanation of reality is perpetually defended such that maturity is left unconsidered. "In natural religion man addresses himself to an object directly antagonistic to the original will and sense of religion . . . he places above himself what he would like to have below himself; he serves what he wishes to govern, adores what in reality he abhors, entreats for assistance that against which he seeks assistance."[55] Either gods are (1) a projection of an individual of an ideal cosmic Father or (2) the projection of a collective into a single consciousness, but however we formulate the projection theory, the idea persists that theology is an ambiguous (1) representative or (2) representation. Psychoanalysis views these latter two terms as very different categories.

> A certain void is always to be preserved, which has nothing to do with the content, neither positive nor negative, of demand. The disruption wherein anxiety is evinced arises when this void is totally filled in.[56]

53. Feuerbach, *Essence of Religion*, 3.
54. Ibid., 15.
55. Ibid., 36.
56. Lacan, *Anxiety*, 65.

The relationship between drive, representation, and representatives are best explored in a story from Freud about his grandson. The child was entertaining himself with a game, throwing a cotton reel attached to a piece of string. The child would throw the reel shouting *Fort!* (gone) and pull it back shouting *Da!* (here). This game was only played while the mother was out of the room, indicating the infant was experiencing anxiety over the loss of the mother and was distracting himself with the game. Now, the worst versions of misapplied analysis might suggest that the cotton reel was acting as a *representation* for the absent mother. But this is not at all the case, for direct links do not always indicate a simple metaphor. What was happening here is properly called repression. The child did not imagine that the cotton reel as a replacement for the mother—the child was perfectly well aware that the mother was not present. Instead the cotton reel served as a representative *in the place of* an actual representation (*Vorstellungrepräsentanz*). The infant surely still felt the anxiety-inducing lack of the mother, but the reel was a symbol that covered over (rather than filled) a void.

There is nothing more dangerous than approaching a void.[57]

Repression is one of four vicissitudes Freud explains, the other three being sublimation, reversal into an opposite, and turning around upon the subject.[58] On Freud's account, when two drives are in conflict, e.g., the infant's desire for the mother and also desire for security in her absence, one drive must take a vicissitude so that the other can directly express itself. Though the unconscious is not strictly composed of repressed drives, all drives undergoing a vicissitude become unconscious.[59] Sublimation and repression are the two we are concerned with in theology. Sublimation is a transformation of the drive into a new activity, and as Lacan adamantly and routinely emphasizes, this process of transformation or redirection is carried out entirely without repression. The common example of the priest or nun whose sexuality has been euphorically redirected into divine servitude shows us exactly how sublimation happens. But should the sublimation of sexuality fail, repression of drives will step in to regulate psychic conflict (often returning the repressed in scandal). On the other hand, repression differs from sublimation by working as a two-phased process. In the

---

57. Lacan, *Psychoses*, 201.

58. Freud, "Instincts and Their Vicissitudes," 569–70.

59. Freud, "Ego and the Id," 631.

primary phase, the drive to be repressed stalls in the unconscious while another drive proceeds and manifests itself. This means that the repressed drive has not transformed into new activity but instead remains operative in some latent form that we should be able to observe shortly. So in order to keep the drive unconscious, a secondary process of repression creates a derivative idea/action to cover over lack.

Derivatives from repression are roughly analogous to economic derivatives. The stock market collapse at the beginning of the Great Recession emerged from subprime mortgage defaults, but the situation was exacerbated when mortgage defaults triggered credit default swaps. These secondary derivatives created a liability that far exceeded the actual value of the mortgages. The ballooning effect of these credit default swaps overwhelmed a bank's ability to repay. The whole scheme was entirely Imaginary—promises on paper derived from money that would not exist—but the exposed a fundamental crisis in Symbolic capital relations. The market experienced a vivid return of the repressed and could not account for the crisis in its network. Unfortunately, irresolvable crises do not always lead to reorientation. The post-crash recovery did little more than legislate small regulatory changes that protected the economic antagonisms they meant to address. And just as derivatives continue to trade in high volume after the market crash, we cannot help but defend and depend upon the derivatives that repression creates for us. Often the idea that most needs to die is what we defend because of the void it covers over.

The drive-conflict conception of repression is Freud's. Thought he does not make his difference explicit, Lacan appears to have a slightly different take. The lack that must be covered over is there from our earliest months, and the secondary process of repression can initiate derivative behaviors without any drive conflict. For Lacan, the fundamental human lack appears more closely tied to the Oedipal conflicts of alienation under the Law and separation from the (lost) object of affection. Alienation and separation initiate our desire for something that can make us whole, something that can never be found because it never existed. But why should the non-existent ideal stop our frantic search? This is my interpretation of Lacan, but the reader should understand Lacan is criticized (perhaps rightly) for seeing *lack* as the fundamental human condition.

COGNATES FOR A VOID AND THEOLOGICAL CATHEXIS

Religion in all its forms consists of avoiding this emptiness.[60]

Theology is at its best when it acknowledges itself as a nexus around a void. What makes religion so interesting from the perspective of psychoanalysis is how it freely oscillates between the frustrated state of repression and the ecstasy of sublimation. One of the things that draws me to study theology (particularly in its less confessional and more radical forms) is that it is a discourse around the periphery of no-(particular)-thing. Theology is like a missing hub of a wheel that only acquires meaning through the cognate fields stretching out like spokes from a center. In addition to historical theologies, the spokes are called hermeneutics and literary theory, politics and economics, gender and queer studies, and a host of others, one of which is psychoanalysis. Psychoanalysis too has its cognate fields (anthropology, mythology, psychology of religions, grammar, poetics)[61] without which the theory would have nothing to say.

Theology, if it desires to speak anything worth hearing, must embrace its precariously obsessional position at the event horizon of the unconscious. Just as art must embrace its hysterical deception of the viewer—for to clarify the proper interpretation too far will cheapen it to propaganda—theology should analyze everything, precisely because it is no-thing. It can only accomplish this task by provocation, which is always a matter of cathexis.

Anger is one avenue to produce cathexis. The parable of the good Samaritan, so universally misunderstood to bear nothing but a command to help those in distress, evokes compassion in modern readers where it would have produced laughter or hatred in its original hearers. On a closer reading, the whole parable seems nothing more than a lengthy a set-up for Jesus to ask the teacher of the law who the protagonist was. We can imagine the seething expert unwilling to concede the word Samaritan, opting instead to shrug of the answer as "the one who had mercy." Is not the parable a truncation of the book of Jonah? In a story where political aspirations are normally lost for the fanciful big fish, Jonah was sent to call Israel's most savage enemy to repentance. Rather than kill the prophet, the king immediately called the nation to repentance and humbled himself before Jonah's God, which of course did nothing but enrage Jonah. Just as the parable of

60. Lacan, *Ethics of Psychoanalysis*, 130.
61. Lacan, *Écrits*, 238.

the Samaritan was told to provoke a hearer, the parable of the repenting Assyrians was told to provoke the Israelite reader. But the provocation only works by exploiting the cathexis between the hearer and the bad-object.

Cathexis invests an object with meaning. Investment may quickly turn itself into ego-cathexis, where we narcissistically attach ourselves to something we cannot imagine being without. We love but do not always know why we love. We hate but do not always have a reasonable explanation. There can be ambivalence between the two,[62] which is due not to an instability in the subject's psyche but instead due to each being a product of a primary cathexis process. It is only after we invest something with meaning that the it becomes good or bad.

Empedocles suggested God must have the most sublime ignorance of all, for God does not know what it is to hate a person. Christianity saw the lack of hate as a sign of love, but Lacan countered, "It is here that analysis reminds us that one knows nothing of love without hate."[63] It is rather difficult to feel justified in our protest when the Other is impassive at best, loving at worst. To feel anger but receive none in return, or to protest without being heard, leads us to the embarrassments of guilt or apathy. One theme throughout this book is that society (particularly within political and theological domains) does need more rage. Our rage should be directed at ideas that simply do not work, or worse, actively cause immense harm.

> The misfortune of Christ is explained to us by the idea of saving men. I find, rather, that the idea was to save God by giving a little presence and actuality back to that hatred of God regarding which we are, and for good reason, rather indecisive.[64]

Is it hyperbolic to suggest Lacanian atonement requires hate every bit as much as it requires love? Atonement theories occupy a peculiar space in Christian theology. Ransom, substitution, and moral exemplar theories (and the numerous derivations of these three) aim to provide an answer a question the early church never saw fit to clarify, namely, as Saint Anselm put it, why the God-man? The ransom theory gave us a devil to rally against, substitution a fixed mechanism on which to depend, and the exemplar a figure to emulate. Substitutionary views in particular are vehemently defended as a tribal signifier, but surely all conceptions of atonement

62. Lacan, *Ethics of Psychoanalysis*, 309. See also Freud, "Ego and the Id," 647.

63. Lacan, *Encore*, 91.

64. Ibid., 98.

demonstrate a level of metaphysical speculation that takes us well beyond the realm of concretized significance. To move only a step forward from Lacan's atonement-as-hatred, I suggest we view atonement as a fetish. The arbitrary fetish object is what the drive aims to encircle, but it did not initially set the drive into motion. Likewise, Christian theology existed well before modern concepts of atonement and will continue to exist long after conceptions pass out of popular appeal. Surely all belief is fetishistic, but atonement occupies a fetish primacy; it part of a signifying chain, and as such the fetish always means something different that what it says.

I wrote previously of the paradigmatic shift, the chipping away of a paradigm that nevertheless remains essentially stable until a precise moment when we lose the ability to believe in a singular point that (in retrospect) turned out to support our entire paradigm. The point may be exposed through the sarcastic joke or the flash of anger, but how are we to know what will provide the kick-start to see what was before us? We can never predict what that point of singular importance will be, but it is there. It is there because our ego has cathected onto a particular point, subsumed it into the network of our identity, and now cannot let go of it. When rational debate merely raises the defense mechanisms, sometimes the de-cathexis process needs the circumventing kick-start of a joke or parable. Whatever the case, it is altogether unnerving to realize that our beliefs choose us, and we are subjugated by an ethical paradox.

Chapter 3

Paradoxes of Law and the Ethics of Psychoanalysis

> Not to recognize the filiation or cultural paternity that exists be-
> tween Freud and a new direction of thought—one that is apparent
> at the break which occurred toward the beginning of the sixteenth
> century . . . constitutes a fundamental misunderstanding of the
> kind of problems Freud's intellectual project addresses.[1]

> The ordinary man cannot imagine this Providence in any other
> form but that of a greatly exalted father . . . The whole thing is so
> patently infantile, so incongruous with reality, that to one whose
> attitude to humanity is friendly it is painful to think that the great
> majority of mortals will never be able to rise above this view of
> life.[2]

I F OUR DESIRE IS actually the desire of the Other, therapy concludes when
we realize the big Other does not exist. We have all sat across from a
friend as she agonizes over a decision to be made based on what a parent
will think, falsely believing not only that (1) the parent's interest in her life
is conditional on a certain course of action but also, and more importantly,
(2) that she is actually trying to please a parent in the first place.[3] The truth

---

1. Lacan, *Ethics of Psychoanalysis*, 97.

2. Freud, *Civilization and Its Discontents*, 23.

3. This example was inspired by a talk Slavoj Žižek delivered some years ago in
New York. It has continued to be a most helpful example of the survival of the big Other's

is that if the parent were to suddenly die, our friend would be no less bound to the parent's approval. As Friedrich Nietzsche wrote, "Our faith in others betrays in what respect we would like to have faith in ourselves,"[4] and is this not precisely what we see with the idealization of an Other whose security is just out of reach. In the case of a parent's death, the language would change, that is to say, one signifier would be replaced with another at the Imaginary tier, but the big Other remains firmly in place. More likely, the death of the Father would make the injunction to obey even more pronounced.

Let us take an example not original to Lacan (but famous in psychoanalytic circles) to describe the demand of the big Other. A man was confined to a psychiatric ward with the paralyzing conviction that he was nothing more than a seed. After a while the delusions subsided, and he was cleared for release. Then upon leaving the clinic, the patient ran terrorized back to his psychiatrist screaming that there was a chicken outside. Disappointed, the psychiatrist explained again to the patient that he was not a seed to be eaten. Of course, the patient replied, he knew this—but would the chicken know? Is this ridiculous structure of displaced belief not exactly what underlies most of the decisions that land us in therapy? Of course we know nobody is compelling us to continually react in such a way, but we fear a nebulous judgment if we were to change.

> We know God is dead . . . However, the next step is that God himself doesn't know that. And one may suppose that he never will know it because he has always been dead . . . *jouissance* still remains forbidden as it was before, before we knew that God was dead.[5]

"The big Other does not exist" is not an empirical claim. The psychoanalytic implication goes much further, delving into the dregs of the unconscious from which our symptoms manifest a fundamental pathology. Psychoanalytic theology interrogates the gods within the three registers while managing to say nothing of value for the metaphysical realities beyond the psyche. It can do this legitimately because reality *qua* reality only begins to matter to us when it enters the Real. We may consciously "know" that the parent is dead, that the gods are dead, or that we are not a seed, but does the big Other know? Until the big Other realizes it does not exist, we remain beholden to its ideologically operative fold.

---

injunctions even after the death of its ego-object manifestations.

4. Nietzsche, "Thus Spoke Zarathustra," 168.

5. Lacan, *Ethics of Psychoanalysis*, 184.

DOSTOEVSKY'S GRAND INQUISITOR

The Brothers Karamazov displayed this mix of egos and big Other fragmented between three brothers and their father Fyodor. The father was pure id—hostile, promiscuous, a scoundrel—and the passionate and manipulating aspects of his personality were divided among two of his sons, the foolishly brash Dmitry and the calculating Ivan. As it went, Dmitry's personality most reflected the father's and erupted into intense family hostility. Just before the murder of the father, Ivan, an atheist whose cunning wit had gained him a reputation as an ecclesiologist, discussed in a dark tavern a parable with the youngest brother, the novice monk Alexie. The story of the Grand Inquisitor suggested a counter-narrative of the church where God was long ago realized to be dead but nevertheless propped up by the priests to keep the social order in place.

Throughout the plot, the Fyodor suggested that if his son Ivan did not believe in God, then anything would be permissible to him. When the father was murdered, the town needed to decide responsibility: the foolish Dmitry, who had openly stated his intention to kill, or the cynical Ivan who believed himself held to no higher standard? The monk Alexie functioned as the one-half of the superego for the family, which cleared all ethical decisions under the son's advice. Concordantly, he would lose that status should his faith wane. Or perhaps it is more appropriate to say that Alexie must not commit the blasphemy of publicly avowing his doubts, for he clearly had them in private. Ivan functioned as the other half of the superego, for where Alexie was compassionate Ivan was rational. Toward the end of the lengthy novel, Dosteovsky let the reader in on a perspective previously withheld: Ivan had been descending into psychosis the entire time. The fiction of careful rationality was propped up by his conversations with a delusional counterpart whenever the family was out of sight.

> As you know, [Fyodor's] son Ivan leads the latter into those audacious avenues taken by the thought of the cultivated man, and in particular, he says, if God doesn't exist . . . then everything is permitted. Quite evidently, a naive notion, for we analysts know full well that if God doesn't exist, then nothing at all is permitted any longer. Neurotics prove that to us every day.[6]

The Grand Inquisitor must keep the ruse up, because as Freud told us, the loss of society's highest ideal is the loss of society as such. The interesting

6. Lacan, *Ego in Freud's Theory*, 128.

thing about Dmitry's parable was that it was not at all clear, in the case that it were true, whether it would be preferable to expose the ruse. To adopt the Symbolic is to enter the realm of the social. To be a normally well-adjusted neurotic citizen requires a dependence on the Other's demands. The scoundrel father believed God was needed to regulate society, and the atheistic prodigy essentially concluded the same. Dostoevsky's story provided Lacan a way to think about the needs of the neurotic without saying anything at all about the implications for the Other in reality as such.

THE IDIOT KING AND THE CENSOR

> If the King of England is an idiot, then everything is permitted . . . This may seem funny to you. but I want it to seem tragic . . . Man is always in the position of never completely understanding the law, because no man can master the law of discourse in its entirety.[7]

Lacan explicated Dostoevsky's story with the old taboo against calling one's king an idiot. The prohibitory law always contains an element of ambiguity created on the one hand by the penalty for transgression and on the other by the probability we will not be caught. Under the Gaze, we are never sure how we measure up or when the moment of judgment will come. We censor our speech in pleasant company so often not because we know we necessarily *will* offend but because there is a *possibility* we would offend. The Other might be dead and not know it, but the Other may also simply be an idiot. The figure of the idiot king provided innumerable plots with a condition where a character (1) might be punished under the strictest terms if caught while (2) knowing the scheme will almost certainly succeed. The certainty of being caught would produce anxiety; we would simply decline to participate. It is precisely when we *probably* will not be caught that we feel far more anxious.

Michel Foucault described the indirect control of anxiety through the nature of surveillance in Jeremy Bentham's panopticon.[8] The prison was designed as a series of circular floors stacked around a single guard tower. Each floor was constructed one cell thick, with one barred window facing out to the world and another facing inward toward the guard tower, ensuring that each prison cell is fully illuminated. Whether the central tower houses ten guards or one, the prisoner would constantly face the chance of

7. Ibid.
8. Foucault, *Discipline and Punish*, 200–228.

a watchful eye. We could imagine the prison carrying on in orderly fashion even if the number of guards behind the darkened glass was zero. The point was not simply that the prisoner could never escape; the point was that the prisoner no longer even tried. Since we are uncertain, we censor, not because we *must* but because it is possible that we *might* need to censor.

> That is censorship in so far as there can never be any relation with the law in its entirety, since the law is never completely made one's own. Censorship and super-ego are to be located in the same register as that of the law.[9]

The figures of the idiot king or the petulant dictator show the effect of legal liminality. We are under judgment at any moment, but we probably have nothing to fear. Primitive death penalties for royal insults covered a great many other things as well that could cause one to lose one's head, so the people learned to censor their speech beyond what was required. This problem returns in our age of mass surveillance and meta-data. We know our online activity is surveilled and that in all likelihood nobody cares about us. Nevertheless, the possibility of surveillance and our uncertainty of where protected speech crosses into sedition requires the conscientious person to censor herself. The effect of censorship is to draw attention to the fact that the ideological king really is an idiot.

THE OBSCENE EXCESS-SUPPLEMENT

Law holds an inherent, perverse ambiguity over our heads when liminality becomes adopted into the superego. Žižek explains this liminal excess with the example of a child who is assured she is not required to visit a grandparent, but then again a good child would want to do so. She will desire to test the parent's word, perhaps briefly protesting, but will eventually self-regulate and submit to expectations. Supposed freedom to choose shows the bipolarity always latent in Law: the supplemental injunction to regulate behavior even when it is not explicitly required and the excessive impulse to do the opposite, to transgress the Law. Law always contains this structure of what Žižek calls the obscene excess-supplement of the superego: (1) the Law commands x, (2) with its ambiguity expecting us to self-regulate beyond the explicit demand ($x+$), and (3) a supplemental injunction demands the opposite ($x-$). The equation balances out: Law normally does not require

9. Lacan, *Ego in Freud's Theory*, 130.

absolute adherence but merely approximation, and this structure crafts the superego into a code of injunctions and corresponding excess-supplements.

Žižek's *Parallax View* contains the clearest example of an obscene excess-supplement through examining the Abu Ghraib scandal.[10] The specter of war crimes—which rightly could have implicated the lowliest private to the highest levels of the administration—was only beginning to surface by the time news broke of brazen sexual abuse among other methods of torture. What was the administration to do with this news? Sexual humiliation was authorized up to a point by Justice Department memos and regularly deployed at black sites and Guantanamo, but the specific use of rape or the covering of prisoners in feces was not officially condoned. The timing of this scandal, concurrent with growing public awareness of Guantanamo, was fortunate for the White House. Abuse authorized and regularly used at Guantanamo and CIA black sites far superseded the localized and sporadic abuses at Abu Ghraib, but (since photographs produce higher public outrage) Abu Ghraib became a fetish to be disavowed. The scandal in one location provided a way to ignore the prevalence of similar tactics everywhere else, allowing the administration to declare the problem was only "a few bad apples." Even that term itself has an endearing element that suppresses its implications, for when one hears "bad apples" one does not immediately make the connection to rape, torture, and in some cases the murder of prisoners. The euphemism functioned in the same way that "enhanced interrogation technique" disavowed the rather simple truth of what it meant to enhance interrogation.

But, Žižek asks, at what point are "bad apples" symptomatic of something else? Let us take the counterfactual and imagine there was never any authorization of torture in any form: would this have made the administration innocent? If we dispatch young soldiers to a dark prison secluded from media on the other side of the world to extract information from targets portrayed as vile, culturally backwards, sub-human, etc., is not the Law also saying "This far, no further—but do whatever you must!"? Law is necessarily complex, ambiguous, and obscene. The human being's desire is whatever the big Other desires, thus the only solution to this enslavement is to cancel the operative power of the Other. The overt command always has a wink and a nod, and because of this we intuitively understand that organizations are responsible for a culture of corruption even where no corrupt command was given for an specific action.

10. Žižek, *Parallax View*, 366–70.

DECALOGUE

> [The Ten Commandments] display the range of what are prop-
> erly speaking our human actions. In other words, we spend our
> time breaking the ten commandments, and that is why society is
> possible.[11]

It is indeed difficult to conceive of a world in which a commandment against coveting could proceed in the order of house-wife-donkey.[12] The commandments, Lacan claims, can be read as a list of our most rigorously concealed desires: if we must be told not to lie, is it not the case that lying is one of our deepest wishes?[13] Equivocation between a wife and a donkey suggests far more than cultural patriarchy; the commandment hints at the more fundamental egoist attachment to prohibited objects. In purely Freudian terms, whether the object-libido is directed at the neighbor's house, his wife, or his donkey, the attachment the subject feels to objects he cannot have is structurally identical regardless of the variable object selected. Whether we need to lie or not, our tendency is to deceive and covet because the Law says we cannot deceive or covet.[14] We deceive not in spite of the taboo against deception but precisely because deception is taboo. The same holds for violence, adultery, respecting one's parents, or resting one day in seven. The experience of object-cathexis here is no more or less arbitrary than whether the neighbor will be loved or hated.

> This [Thing] was there from the beginning, that it was the first
> thing that separated itself from everything the subject began to
> name and articulate, that the covetousness that is in question is
> not addressed to anything that I might desire but to a thing that is
> my neighbor's Thing.[15]

The desired object is only a thing we desire because it bears a resemblance to the Thing. Whether by positive or negative injunction, we learn what to desire at the Imaginary register through the mediation of the Symbolic. Saint Paul's innovation was to realize the big Other does not exist, that is to say, to cancel the Law's operative power. For Paul, sin was created precisely by exporting our responsibilities onto the divine Symbolic register.

11. Lacan, *Ethics of Psychoanalysis*, 96.
12. Ibid., 82.
13. Ibid.
14. Ibid., 83.
15. Ibid.

The oral traditions of Jewish Law often appear excessive to the Christian reader, but there is a coherent logic: if the Law occupies such a primary position in the organization of society, no amount of derivative protections around the taboo will seem too far. In our enlightened era, no longer appealing to sacred books for our ethics and laws, our naïve deontology or consequentialism still tends to maintain the same dependence on the big Other, regardless of whether or not we believe our Law was written by a Law-giver. And it is no mystery why we do this, frightening as it is to think of ethics as relatively baseless and ultimately consisting merely of social negotiations. But while secular varieties of deontology are more appealing in a pluralistic society, they are fated to the same indefensible foundationalism as divine deontology. The ethics of psychoanalysis locates the central antagonism not as id-against-ego but instead within the Symbolic itself. Put differently, the problem is not the flesh resisting righteousness but instead the very notion that one can be righteous. The notion of righteousness is an ideal ego that becomes grafted into the superego, and from this moment on the perpetual judgment becomes automatic. This is the line of thought that travels from Saint Paul to Freud, and certainly from Luther to Lacan.

Saint Paul claimed not that the Law merely *defined* sin but that the Law actively *created* sin. Lacan found this analogous to what he observed in his analysands, and he formulated the same theme as such: the prohibition of the superego generates desire. Whatever gets itself labeled as sin can usually be formulated as an excess of id. For example, the aggression that results in misdirected violence today is the same aggression that natural selection cultivated in our ancestors who could not have survived without it. But to formulate sin as an excess of id or the flesh does not go all the way to Paul's radical claim that Law itself creates sin. One cannot read Paul or Freud and conclude that the harmful act is simply and only an excess of the id. Again, we must remember that Lacan locates the drive specifically as a function of the Symbolic, and that drive acquires excessive enjoyment not from directly acquiring object but by endlessly encircling the object. To directly acquire provides pleasure but not the excessive allure of *jouissance*. Once the commandments are broken, the allure of transgressing the prohibition dissolves into mundanity.

> Luther writes of the following—God's eternal hatred of men, not simply of their failures and the works of their free will, but a hatred that existed even before the world was created. You see that there

are reasons why I advise you to read religious authors from time to time.[16]

This is because the Thing is in the Real and cannot be captured because it does not exist. The Real, as we have said, is pre-symbolic, traumatic, that which enters our world and compels a response even before we know what we are engaging. The Thing suffers from being signified,[17] degraded by definition and concretization as a lesser object to capture. But the futile effort of the drive sets all of life in motion on the seductive promise that finding the Thing would make our lives whole.[18] Lacan reformulates Paul's premise: it is the Law that creates the *Thing*, the Thing deceives us into thinking it will make us whole, and most importantly, the Law prohibits us from acquiring the Thing. Law creates *jouissance* by installing a limit, for it is the limit that elevate the thing to a Thing of fantasy.

This chapter draws primarily from a seminar entitled *The Ethics of Psychoanalysis*, the irony being that very little is said toward constructing an ethics. Lacan was quite clearly opposed to a return to unbridled instinct,[19] but he also opposed traditionally deontological social ethics.[20] We could assume his hesitancies against utilitarian ethics as well (provided there is any truth to notion of a death drive). John Stuart Mill took it for granted that human beings seek happiness. The field of therapy only exists because we do not. We have an immensely creative death drive with incalculable derivations of self-destructive behaviors and repetitions. In the political field, "there is no satisfaction for the individual outside of the satisfaction of all,"[21] but what satisfaction means is always being reformulated, shaped by the values of the fool or the knave. Perhaps this leaves the very Aristotelean Lacan open to a highly nuanced virtue ethics, advocating a mean between extremes, but even this would leave Lacan open to charges of nihilism or crypto-deontology. But Lacan's argument on morality is not so different that what we observe in economies; ethics cannot be reducible to social constraints because of the wide and fundamental difference between instinctual needs and desires of the drive.[22] All that can be said is what

16. Ibid., 97.
17. Ibid., 118.
18. Ibid., 75.
19. Ibid., 311.
20. Ibid., 314.
21. Ibid., 292.
22. Ibid., 225.

morality is most certainly not: simply submitting ourselves uncritically to the big Other's desire.

THE PARADOXES OF ETHICS OR HAVE YOU ACTED IN CONFORMITY WITH YOUR DESIRE?

This question (the title of the final chapter in the seminar on ethics) confronts the reader with the ultimate question for psychoanalytic ethics and psychoanalytic theology alike. The paradox is that the ethical requires submission to the frustrating demands of the big Other. Like any economy, ethics is a communal decision about how to divide resources among the interests of others. The ethical paradox is not unlike Freud's view of therapy, being that we lift abject misery to ordinary unhappiness. The question of either (1) submission to a paradox or (2) acting in conformity with our desire is another way of asking whether theology is instinct or drive. We frequently hear religion foreclose on ethical considerations on the grounds that the big Other already made up its mind; no reconsideration is permitted. Anything less than full submission to the normative injunction is precarious, potentially horrific, and certainly heretical. There is never guarantee it will end well when people start making decisions. But again, as Heschel wrote, it is hypocrisy—not heresy—that leads to spiritual decay.

We are not to regress to pure id, as if paradise were a social psychosis. We are also not to export responsibility onto the plane of the Symbolic, as if fidelity requires the enslavement of the obsessive neurotic. We are not to evade the big questions so as to postpone our confrontation with the pure truth that we tend to repeat what is not working, as if security can be found in hysteria. We can only offer a caution: who is asking us to see the world this way? And why are we so eager to submit to the Other's self-proclaimed representative, whether in the form of a person or an ideology?

> The saint doesn't really see himself as righteous, which doesn't mean that he has no ethics. The only problem for others is that you can't see where it leads him . . . The more saints, the more laughter; that's my principle, to wit, the way out of capitalist discourse— which will not constitute progress, if it happens only for some.[23]

Lacan concludes with four propositions on ethics. First, all we are guilty of is giving ground relative to our desire (that is, living for an(O)

23. Lacan, *Television*, 16.

ther's desire). Second, society idolizes the hero, who is nothing more than someone society can betray with impunity. Third, not everyone can become a hero, for the ordinary person who is betrayed will give up on desire and return to the service of goods. Is this not our tempting position if life stabilizes into routine at the cost of its *raison d'être*? Lastly, access to what we desire must be paid for with the price of metonymy. Acquiring or losing what we desire changes us in ways we may never become aware.

In Gospel of Luke, the parable of the shrewd steward provided an excursus on the paradoxical Laws of Heaven. The story concerned an accounts manager who faced an immanent accusation of mismanagement and calculated his chances would be better if he were to cheat the master in order to find favor with those indebted to the house. The steward contacted debtors and settled accounts for a fraction of what each owed the master. One can only serve Yahweh or Mammon, but why not play by the rules of Mammon for friendship? How remarkable, Lacan observed, "the best way to achieve salvation for one's soul is to embezzle the funds one is in charge of."[24]

Morality begins with desire, both as a universalized axiom and as an simple object we aim for without quite knowing the goal.[25] Sublime wisdom and full hedonism alike fascinate with a morality opposed to (or outside the scope of) the reality principle, but we cannot quite say what it is about the *beyond* of the reality principle that so intrigues.[26] The laws of desire are the Laws of Heaven.[27] And every act of desire inscribes another tally mark against us in the big Other's Great Book of Debts.[28] This is the paradox of the big Other: its command enjoy, but we shall be judged for our enjoyment.[29]

> The perpetual reproach that is born at that moment . . . remains fundamental in the structure of the subject. It is this imaginary father and not the real one which is the basis of the providential image of God. And the function of the superego in the end, from

24. Lacan, *Ethics of Psychoanalysis*, 96.
25. Ibid., 70.
26. Ibid., 109.
27. Ibid., 325.
28. Ibid., 177.
29. Ibid., 192.

its final point of view, is hatred for God, the reproach that God has handled things so badly.[30]

What we shall covet is always a Thing mediated by its current status as our neighbor's thing. Like a rabbit drawn from a hat, the object we covet is Imaginary and interchangeable for anything else.[31] We did not notice we needed the *thing* until it became a *Thing*, which it became the moment the big Other said: Do you see this?—you cannot have it. The command to love our neighbor raises protests of envy, ensuing criminality raises the question of the Sovereign Good, and the failure to find the Sovereign Good leads the regressive vanity of false goods.[32] Whether psychotic, neurotic, or perverse, the analysand must eliminate her demands for false gods.

30. Ibid., 308.
31. Ibid., 293.
32. Ibid., 300.

Chapter 4

Psychopathology
Psychosis, Neurosis, and Perversion

Now when the child grows up and finds that he is destined to remain a child for ever, and that he can never do without protection against unknown and mighty powers, he invests these with the traits of the father-figure; he creates for himself the gods, of whom he is afraid, whom he seeks to propitiate, and to whom he nevertheless entrusts the task of protecting him.[1]

Ignorance, indifference, an averting of the eyes may explain beneath what veil this mystery still remains hidden. But for whoever is capable of turning a courageous gaze towards this phenomenon . . . we try to find evidence for the presence of the desire of this Other that I call here the dark God.[2]

IF WE LIVE IN the aftermath of the word's entry into the world, the unconscious will demand a hearing. We negotiate our experiences through the unconscious schemas placed upon us for the most part by the time we utter our first words, and not unlike Job, we are forever in the position of an ego demanding the big Other give account for the Real irruption of trauma. Psychopathology is a universal phenomenon, inflicting its vicissitudes and symptoms on each of us with varying degrees of compulsion, but crafting most of us as neurotic, a few of us as perverse, and fewer still as fully

1. Freud, *Future of an Illusion*, 42.
2. Lacan, *Four Fundamental Concepts of Psychoanalysis*, 275.

psychotic. As one of Lacan's students put it, "What happens in one's guts is unnameable, but it ends up being named."[3]

I should readily admit this will be the densest of chapters in this book, but I offer this theoretical exposition of individual psychopathology in order to practically explore social psychopathology in the following chapters. Key to understanding psychopathology is that it designates a particular relationship of the conscious ego to the unconscious totality of the subject's existence. Jungian theory and its followers developed something roughly analogous with personality types, but Freudian/Lacanian psychopathology engages a much more specific and fundamental relationship. If the unconscious is structured like a language, we could say psychopathology is about how our conscious relates to symbolism both at conscious and unconscious levels. And since religion is symbolism, psychopathology has a largely untapped capability for exploring the different ways we relate to religious thought.

PSYCHOSIS AND THE SECRETARIES TO THE INSANE

It is said that the analyst is a secretary to the insane.[4] Hallucination is a synthesis of imagination and trauma.[5] Psychosis, whether in temporary states of delusion or long-term schizoid conditions, is rarely the default psychopathology a person adopted as a child. It is unique among the psychopathologies as a descent later in life. There is an old saying in psychoanalytic circles that it takes a good three generations to produce a true psychotic, which emphasizes the family patterns of abuse, neglect, or addiction involved in shaping the individual. This inter-generational pattern is by no means a strict rule since the onset of psychosis often inflicts itself with little warning, but the saying rightly promotes psychosis as a long-term degradation of the Symbolic. Psychosis is inherently unstable, not just in its behavioral manifestations but also in the flux of extremity with which it afflicts an individual. Lacan's seminar on the psychoses even cautions his students that an improper interpretation during analysis can trigger an otherwise neurotic subject into a psychotic state. Psychosis is always triggered by something, and that something can be new or long hidden in the unconscious, lying dormant until it can rear its head.

3. Lacan, *Ego in Freud's Theory*, 216.
4. Lacan, *Psychoses*, 206.
5. Lacan, *Freud's Papers on Technique*, 104.

Psychosis is the "the symbolic's failure to overwrite the imaginary,"[6] the lack of alienation into language, and the totalizing non-experience of the big Other's injunctions to comply with normative social behavior. Put differently, when we see an individual frantically arguing with an imaginary friend, it is not that she is aware in the same sense we are that she is talking to herself or that she believes this behavior to be socially acceptable. Instead, she is wholly without the big Other's regulating injunction against this behavior. She is not altogether without some element of the Symbolic (as demonstrated by her use of language, compliance with rudimentary social norms, etc.), but specific elements of the big Other are missing or non-functioning. In neurotic and perverse subjects, the conscious is on display and the unconscious is hidden; in psychosis, this is reversed.[7] The clinical term for the collapse of the Symbolic is *foreclosure*. Unlike repression, where drives are (1) repressed into the unconscious and (2) proceed to return symptoms or derivative behaviors, foreclosure closes its ears, collapsing altogether the logic of the unconscious. And whatever is foreclosed in the Symbolic will reappear with brute force in the Real.[8]

> We know that the human child cannot well complete its development towards culture without passing through a more or less distinct phase of neurosis. This is because the child is unable to suppress by rational mental effort so many of those instinctual impulses which cannot later be turned to account, but has to check them by acts of repression, behind which there stands as a rule an anxiety motive.[9]

Before the mirror stage, an infant has not yet developed the neural capacity to think of itself as an individual. The stage at which the infant understands the object-permanence of something hidden from its view comes roughly at the same time when the reflection in the mirror can be recognized as the same self viewing the mirror. The mirror stage is the emergence of the self-aware ego, but it is interesting to notice what the infant does the moment he recognizes his reflection. What does the infant always do?—she turns around to the mother, every time, as if we depend on the big Other's ratification from our earliest moments of awareness.[10] The

6. Fink, *Clinical Introduction to Lacanian Psychoanalysis*, 87.

7. Lacan, *Psychoses*, 11.

8. Ibid., 13.

9. Freud, *Future of an Illusion*, 75.

10. Lacan, *Anxiety*, 32.

mirror stage awakens the individualism of the infant, but individualism immediately and curiously requires the big Other's ratification.

Before the awakening of the ego, the infant is essentially pure id acting out of instinct. There is doubtless some level of consciousness, but the capacity necessary to produce anything more necessary than basic needs is not there from the start. As the ego develops the infant quickly learns its caretakers are beings with interests too. This realization that it is not the sole object of affection constitutes the mother side of the Oedipus complex. Lacan calls this phase separation to designate the permanent end of any illusions the infant could have of being forever unified with its caretaker as the sole object of the mother's desire. Alienation, the father side of the complex, quickly ensues with the development of the superego as the child begins to understand there are certain rules it must follow. Alienation inflicts the (1) the sense of loss around which repression-derivatives will emerge and (2) dominance of the signifier. In the introduction, I described separation and alienation as the two reasons we go to therapy.

The resolution of the complex and the conditions of alienation and separation will have permanent ramifications for psychic disposition. Resolution is only a tentative and partial; none of us are ever fully "over" the dispositions created for us in our earliest years, but in well-adjusted neurotic and perverse types, the varied implications of early experiences preset patterns. We do not escape our trauma, but eventually understand traumatic experiences shape us, often for worse, but often as well for the better. The Real becomes signified and grafted into the Symbolic. Psychosis could be conceived as a catastrophic erasure of lines of code within the Symbolic that produces socially unsanctioned behavior.

Lacan always cautioned against understanding too much: it is in understanding that illusion begins to take hold and misdirect our analysis.[11] People (not to mention entire social systems) will always display their problems, but it will not be what they articulate with words. Like the old Cracow joke, there is always a possible feint in the message, and the truth comes through in some inverted formulation.[12] What is understandable is not what is important.[13] What truly needs our attention is what does not work.

11. Lacan, *Psychoses*, 21.

12. Ibid., 37.

13. Ibid., 22.

SCHREBER, PARANOIA, AND FUNDAMENTAL FANTASY

This is never more true than when analyzing the delusions of psychosis, where the "talking cure" fails to work because the unconscious ceased to function like a coherent language. The case study of Judge Schreber and his journals detailing his descent provided Freud a window into hallucinations and delusions of grandeur in progressive psychosis. After a short stay at a mental hospital from 1884–85 due to hypochondriac panic attacks, Schreber displayed no symptoms for eight years. During the latency period, his career flourished and he secured an appointment as Presiding Judge of Appeals at Leipzig. The promotion triggered impostor syndrome anxieties, and his panic attacks returned along with insomnia and hallucination. He recommitted himself to a series of psychiatric clinics until 1901. Two years later, Schreber published his journals detailing his paranoiac experience under the title *Memoirs of My Nervous Illness*.

God prominently occupied the pathological nucleus of Schreber's delusions. The memoir obsesses over the survival of the ego after death, which indicates a progressively acute narcissism functioning as a foundation for delusion. These narcissism-based delusions evolved into a cryptic description of nervous energy emitting "divine rays" (what Schreber called the foundation for souls). He began to believe purely biological activity of human beings would change the nature of God. Freud actually saw in Schreber's idea something analogous to his theory of libidinal cathexis.[14] Or put differently, as is the case with much of religious language, Schreber described something approximating reality through insufficient language.

> In neurosis, inasmuch as reality is not fully rearticulated symbolically into the external world, it is in a second phase that a partial flight from reality, an incapacity to confront this secretly preserved part of reality, occurs in the subject. In psychosis, on the contrary, reality itself initially contains a hole that the world of fantasy will subsequently fill.[15]

Schreber's case includes a bizarre excursus on becoming the wife of God. Homoerotic desire merged with his obsession on the "structure of God" to the point that he could not imagine man as having any purpose outside of being the wife of God.[16] This allows us to introduce an impor-

14. See the account of Schreber in Lacan, *Psychoses*, 25–28.
15. Lacan, *Psychoses*, 45.
16. Ibid., 62.

tant concept in Lacan called the *fundamental fantasy*, which designates how the subject relates to the big Other and the desired object. How the subject relates to the object in behavior is quite different than how the subject imagines the relationship, but codifying and analyzing the subject's fundamental fantasy allows for a more precise analysis of the individual analysand (and in the next chapter, analysis of entire social systems).

Lacan wrote fantasy as a matheme, and the standard matheme for the split subject desiring an object is written ($\$ \diamond a$). The matheme should be read as a relationship between the objects on the left and right, and the diamond designates the reciprocal influence of the two symbols upon each other. The S-barred designates a subject split into conscious and unconscious, but it also designates the constitutive lack driving the desire to recover the imaginary lost object (a). The diamond shows a relationship between the two created by our alienation into language and our separation from the lost object; the a is only a cause of desire once there is a subject desiring it, and the subject is only split through awakening to the idea that something is missing. Lacan seemed to see all secondary fantasies as conscious justifications for the unconsciously fundamental fantasy. Fundamental fantasy is more difficult to discern in psychosis because the unconscious is on full display. We could write Schreber's delusional fantasy as ($a \diamond A$) and read it as Schreber's desire to be the object a for God. There is certainly nothing abnormal about a fantasy in which one person relates to an(O)ther. But the Other in Schreber's case is free-floating, delusional, and ultimately only interested in taking him for a wife. Some element of the Symbolic big Other is functions in psychosis, but it is a highly degraded and unstable version of what operates in the vast majority of us. Something happened that cannot be incorporated into Schreber's Symbolic, "an essential signifier that is unable to be received."[17]

THE END OF (ANTI-)SOCIAL PSYCHOSIS

If we define psychosis as the failure of the Symbolic to overwrite the Imaginary or, alternately, the lack of superego regulation, then it should be clear that psychosis is impossible for a culture to collectively display. A community withstands short bursts of anti-social acts, but being a society requires a social superego—customs, laws, taboos—that restrains its citizens impulses. Freud wrote of "the child's great cultural achievement—the

17. Ibid., 306.

instinctual renunciation . . . which he had made in allowing his mother to go away without protesting."[18] After this moment, and not a moment before, the child enters society by restraining preferred behavior. So just in the way that the pre-mirror stage infant does not have the cognizance needed to recognize a reflection, so our ancestors existed in a type of psychotic, pre-Symbolic state until the level of cognizance reached a social capacity. Prior to the Symbolic, there is only primal chaos.[19]

The myth of the Fall in Genesis tells of the transition to civilization or, alternately, humankind's transition out of psychosis. Religion preceded *homo sapiens*, and the death rituals from which it emerged are analogous to a cultural mirror stage at which point early hominids began to experience emotional distress at the passing of a tribe member. God commanded Adam and Eve to not eat from a specific tree called Knowledge of Good and Evil. The entry of the big Other's injunction exists here not as a systematic codification of rights and wrongs that develop later in the Torah but instead only as a specific injunction *against* knowing right and wrong in the first place.

As we have seen, the prohibition generates the desire. Eve believed she could not even touch the tree, which suggests something about the relationship between taboo and desire. God had only commanded that she not eat, but if the tree marked the singular taboo in the garden, then it is not difficult to imagine why Eve would begin to self-regulate beyond what God required. Recall our discussion of oppressive surveillance and the panopticon prison in the previous chapter. Bentham designed it to make escape impossible, but what Foucault found interesting was that the prisoner self-regulated and no longer even attempted escape. Once a big Other's prohibition grafts itself into place, the subject will begin to guard the taboo object with progressively expansive prohibitions. Upon examination these expanding prohibitions are indefensible, thus once the serpent questioned the derivative rules guarding the tree the original prohibition at the locus of those derivatives lost operative power.

> It has to be said of human psychology what Voltaire used to say about natural history, which was that it's not as natural as all that and that, frankly, nothing could be more anti-natural.[20]

18. Freud, "Beyond the Pleasure Principle," 600.
19. Lacan, *Freud's Papers on Technique*, 79.
20. Lacan, *Psychoses*, 7–8.

Psychopathology

We could imagine that a garden governed only by the pleasure principle, lacking even the civilizing effect of the reality principle, would quickly
unleash the worst aspects of the id without any felt need of restraint. The
paradise would devolve into a murderous hell in short order. Maturity
requires immaturity first; dialectic progress requires clearly established
antagonisms. The speaking serpent offered an opportunity to be like God,
but what the couple received was a superego to shame them. The transgression into knowledge of good and evil stopped short the pure id soon to
be unleashed, and this first transgression was the salvation of the couple
themselves. Was the newly death-bound neurotic couple better off with a
superego? Perhaps so, and certainly civilization could not have arisen without the entry of good and evil, norms and taboos. But repression is never
simply suppression. Repression always returns in an inverted form, and the
id postponed in the mythic parents returned directly as murder in their
children.

NEUROSIS

> Language allows [the neurotic] to regard himself as a stagehand,
> or even the director, of the entire imaginary capture of which he
> would otherwise be nothing more than the living marionette. Fan-
> tasy is the very illustration of this original possibility.[21]

Freud described the obsessive and hysteric forms of neurosis as breaking with reality and substituting reality with a particular fantasy.[22] This is
most people's fundamental disposition toward the world, a fantasy shad-
ing the reality with which we naïvely assume we are interacting. The vast
majority of us fit this category, with the two main subtypes being obsessives and hysterics.[23] Just as the psychotic is constituted by the mechanism
of *foreclosure*, the neurotic is constituted by the mechanism of *repression*.
It is not that neurotics repress so much as repression leads to becoming
neurotic, but the conditioning that comes from continual repression makes

21. Lacan, *Écrits*, 532.

22. Lacan, *Freud's Papers on Technique*, 90.

23. Obsessive and hysteric are generally considered, respectively, masculine and
feminine. I want to acknowledge the serious problems both with the derogatory and
archaic use of the word "hysteric" to refer to a generally female disposition as well as the
problems with expecting to fit a gender binary. Indeed, analysts are quick to point out
that several sessions are needed to make the diagnosis; gender should never determine
the diagnosis. The diagnosis should come strictly from the analysand's fantasy.

69

the neurotic more likely to continue to repress in the future (rather than foreclose or, as we will see with perversion, disavow). We discussed repression in chapter 2, but let us again summarize by saying (1) primary repression displaces one or more drives when there is a conflict of interest that produces anxiety, and (2) secondary repression is the covering-over of this through the production of derivative symptoms/behaviors. A thought that we repress must be at least partly conscious, if only for the briefest moment, but is then denied entrance.[24]

The production of symptoms in secondary repression is the reason Lacan constantly reminds his students that repression and the return of the repressed are the same. If we repress, it inevitably produces symptomatic effects to cover anxiety. Whether we respond to our stress with our gods or our alcohol, the symptomatic derivative is arbitrary. Repression, along with its counterpart vicissitudes (sublimation, reversal into an opposite, and turning around upon the subject), is responsible for most of what is produced in our culture. I say this to emphasize that repression as such is not a bad or unhealthy thing. Freud described repression as the conscious psyche's attempt to keep something far off in the distance.[25] Repression and sublimation produce an elaborate construct of repression-returns, and this is necessary for a functioning society. But those returns begin to lock into repetition, and thus we repeat behaviors and beliefs that do not work. To analyze what is happening in religion, we need to understand (1) how different psychopathologies hear the same message in very different ways and (2) how variances between our psychopathologies produce conflict.

OBSESSIONAL NEUROSIS

> Amid so many seductive, insurgent, and impassive attitudes, we must grasp the anxieties that are bound up with performance, the grudges that do not prevent generosity . . . and the mental infidelities that sustain infrangible loyalties.[26]

The obsessive is enslaved to the big Other. The obsessive develops routines and modes of thought that make repetition function like an autopilot. The obsessive does not want to think of herself as controlled by elements outside of her awareness (commonly denying even the reality

24. Freud, "Repression," 570.
25. Ibid., 569–70.
26. Lacan, *Écrits*, 526–7.

of an unconscious or believing her problems can be interrogated without assistance)[27] and is thus perfectly suited to be controlled by what she excludes from consciousness. The obsessive goes to therapy to regain control over her life and begins, after quickly detailing the situation that brought her there, asks the analyst what she should do, i.e., what does the big Other want me to do? Self-sabotage in obsessives is easily done by maintaining routines that do not work (producing results that are just tolerable enough to merit ignoring) and taking security in obeying the Other, whatever manifestation that Other takes in the obsessive's life. The universal, unconscious desire for repetition functions in a particularly pronounced way for the obsessive's mode of life.

> Am I saying this to explain the difficulty of his desire? No, rather to say that his desire is for difficulty.[28]

> In obsessional neurosis, the object with relation to which the fundamental experience, the experience of pleasure, is organized, is an object which literally gives too much pleasure . . . the behavior of the obsessional reveals and signifies is that he regulates his behavior so as to avoid what the subject often sees quite clearly as the goal and end of his desire."[29]

The obsessive's repetition is organized around the heightened unconscious pleasure of primal trauma.[30] This is not to say that the obsessive realizes what is happening when she exports responsibility for her decisions onto a big Other; quite the opposite, for the obsessional desires to feel in control, and it is for this self-deception of control that the obsessive exports a decision to unconscious repetition. The obsessive's fantasy is "everything for the Other."[31] The defense mechanisms become a rigid frame,[32] locking up the obsessive to guard against the horror of what she cannot allow herself to know. We can see how the obsessive, particularly in extreme cases, would turn out to appear remarkably ethical based on the need to fit within a chain of signifying rules. Duty is keenly felt regardless of

27. Fink, *Clinical Introduction to Lacanian Psychoanalysis*, 130.

28. Lacan, *Écrits*, 529.

29. Lacan, *Ethics of Psychoanalysis*, 53–54.

30. Lacan, *Four Fundamental Concepts of Psychoanalysis*, 69–70.

31. Lacan, *Écrits*, 514.

32. Lacan, *Ethics of Psychoanalysis*, 203.

whether this duty can be fulfilled.[33] And this appearance of acting ethically is highly pronounced, for the obsessive will be quite dependable, but the broader question of what ethics *gets at* from the previous chapter returns with a vengeance for the obsessive. It is not that the obsessive follows the rule for the sake of doing good (though this will be her fantasy) so much as that a rule is followed because submission is the obsessive's comfort. To act unethically would harm the person the obsessive is interacting with, but at a more fundamental level an unethical act would challenge the obsessive's presumptive identity. We see this with distancing behavior, e.g., the apologetic exclamation that acting out was an anomaly. The motivation for what we now apologize for came from somewhere unconscious, which is more us than our conscious façades. But the ego must distance itself from its truth when its truth is found to be grotesque.

> Whatever he tells you, whatever feelings he brings to you, it is always those of someone other than himself. This objectification of himself isn't due to an inclination or to a gift for introspection. It is to the extent that he evades his own desire that all desire to which, were it only ostensibly, he commits himself, will be represented by him as the desire of this other self that is his ego.[34]

The more extreme the case of obsessional neurosis, the more desire is impossible[35] (at least, desire in the direct sense of an ego desiring a lost object). The Lacanian axiom that *our desire is the Other's desire* manifests nowhere more clearly than in the extreme obsessive. The primary fantasy of the obsessive is to imagine she has the type of control the big Other has, and her fantasy life aims to "accentuate the impossibility of the subject vanishing."[36] In a sense, the obsessive fantasy ignores the Other whereas the hysteric's fantasy aims specifically to be the object of the big Other's desire, an object that is always slipping away and leaving the Other unsatisfied. The hysteric is defiant; the obsessive is submissive. Which would a dominant ideology rather have fill its rosters?

---

33. Ibid., 7.
34. Lacan, *Ego in Freud's Theory*, 268.
35. Lacan, *Écrits*, 571.
36. Ibid., 698.

What is the obsessional waiting for? The death of the master. What use does this waiting have for him? It is interposed between him and death. When the master is dead, everything will begin.[37]

The life of the obsessive consists of waiting for the big Other's authorization.[38] The fantasy is that a freedom is found in being directed, and the obsessive that comes to terms with this may fantasize that the death of the Other with its viciously persistent criticism may bring its freedom. Some wish for a parent's approval for the same reason others wish to rid themselves of faith; the Imaginary manifestations of the big Other have no bearing on its continued structure within the neurotic psyche.

If an obsessional tells you that he doesn't care for something or someone, you can take it that it touches him to the quick. When he expresses great indifference, that is when his interest is caught at its maximum.[39]

So how does the obsessive break out of this enslavement? What does it mean for an obsessive to overcome her symptoms and realize the big Other does not exist? Obsessives and hysterics alike raise questions at the level of ego in order to defend a more acute, anxiety-evoking question from rising within the unconscious. Questions are raised so that they are not really raised, and this perpetuates symptomatic repetition.[40] As we discussed with the descent into psychosis, the improperly acute question is always at risk of triggering the obsessional into psychosis. And indeed, especially in religious communities, obsessives can over-identify with language that appears psychotic (especially when it is clear—due to a disparity between word and deed—that the obsessive does not actually believe what she imagines herself to believe). Lacan laments that extreme cases of obsessive neurosis have often been mislabeled as psychosis,[41] which is not so hard too imagine when we see members of a community who display a tunnel vision toward one particularly disruptive idea. The properly acute question can only rise at the moment where the Imaginary is pierced and the obsessive is forced to confront the Symbolic head on.

37. Lacan, *Freud's Papers on Technique*, 286.
38. Ibid., 286.
39. Lacan, *Ego in Freud's Theory*, 269.
40. Lacan, *Psychoses*, 174.
41. Lacan, *Ego in Freud's Theory*, 272.

It isn't by forcing him to abandon his discourse, but by inciting him to follow it through to the terminal stage of its dialectical rigor, that you will be able to get [the obsessive] to understand how he is always frustrated of everything in advance. The more he grants himself things, the more he grants them to the other, to this dead man, and he finds himself eternally deprived of any kind of enjoyment [*jouissance*] in the thing. If he doesn't understand this step, there is no way that you'll ever get yourself out of it.[42]

Lacan seems to argue in therapy something close to what Žižek deploys through over-identification with a pernicious ideology in such a way that the ideology's horrific consequences are put on full display. However problematic an ideology may be, it can maintain popular support so long as its logic is kept at a distance rather than chased to its conclusion. We see this problem all the time in our politics and our religious communities when large sections of a population maintains basically the same political ideology or theology that some derided extremist group maintains, the only difference being that the latter is foolish enough (or perhaps extremists simply have more integrity) to actually say what they believe. The vast distance between overtly hostile patriarchy and patriarchy with a smile can be maintained as long as the hypocrisy is left veiled, and the over-identification of a grotesque ideology combats the acceptably of the smile by saying: you find us repulsive, because we believe your beliefs better than you. In the same way, Peter Rollins observes that it is rarely those who believed too little that leave the church; instead, it is usually those who believed too much. Those who leave are those who cannot hear "Do not worry about this so much!" without protesting in return, "Is none of this serious to you?" The obsessive is particularly prone to this anxiety, but the psyche that produces this antagonism is graciously well-equipped to chase the anxiety to its conclusion, to traverse the fantasy, and thereby leave behind ideologies that do not work. The obsessive that realizes she depends on an Other that does not deserve her loyalty is an obsessive that can begin to reorient her desires and belief toward what works.[43]

---

42. Ibid., 217.
43. Ibid., 269.

HYSTERICAL NEUROSIS

The unconscious reveals itself through its deceptions, and self-deception is the marker the analyst looks for in the case of the hysteric.[44] Whereas the obsessive's desire is felt as impossible, the hysteric's desire is left unsatisfied.[45] Defense mechanisms lead to behavioral repetition, which is kept in place to keep both unconsciously unhappy. We should again clarify that all of these defenses and the goals of repetition are all unconscious; it is not that anyone supposes she would like to be unhappy, but that healing requires far more anxiety than repetition. Because of the basic need for stasis, we sabotage because it is far easier in the short term than therapy.

> So hysteria places us, I would say, on the track of some kind of original sin in analysis. There has to be one.[46]

It was through analyzing hysteria that Freud claimed he discovered the unconscious.[47] Hysterical desire has a less submissive yet equally dependent relationship to the big Other. Freud's famous case of Dora explicated the hysteric's need for an external entity's happiness as a condition for her own. Dora's symptoms arose coeval with her desire for her father to be happy with his new love interest. Dora's desire was to sustain her father's desire.[48] When her father began an affair with the wife of Herr K., Dora seduced Herr K., apparently in order to distract Herr K. from the affair in his home. The dual affairs carried on for some time, but Dora lost all interest in Herr K. at the moment his interest in his wife faded. She was altogether unsatisfied already in her end of the affair with Herr K., but so long as the arrangement between the four of them sustained her father's desire for the wife, Dora was able to sustain her desire for Herr K. (as a substitution for her father's desire for Herr K.'s wife). The end of Herr K.'s desire for his wife triggered several competing anxieties for Dora: the end of the prohibition by the prospect of being in a relationship that would no longer be an affair, the effect the divorce would have for her father's relationship to the wife, and, perhaps most importantly, the inability to accept herself as an object of desire for Herr K. on her own merits.

---

44. Lacan, *Four Fundamental Concepts of Psychoanalysis*, 33.

45. Lacan, *Écrits*, 571.

46. Lacan, *Four Fundamental Concepts of Psychoanalysis*, 12.

47. Ibid., 12.

48. Ibid., 38.

For the obsessive, the axiom *one's desire is the desire of the Other* takes the form complying with the demands of the big Other, molding her desire to fit whatever the Other is perceived to desire. For the hysteric the same axiom inverts in meaning so that her desire is to sustain the desire of the big Other. Likewise, the obsessive is unable to formulate her desire with words if she is unsure of what the big Other desires. The hysteric actively constructs her desire through words. Borderline personality disorder presents an excellent example of hysterical neurosis, inasmuch as the borderline patient actively constitutes new realities through elaborate stories for self-deception, talking herself into narratives. The borderline patient will have no awareness that she does this in order to sabotage her happiness, because the hysteric psyche aims not to get what it desires but to sustain the Other's desire. Whether the borderline is sustaining the desire of a lover or sustaining her desirous position for society, i.e., projecting new versions of herself that make one appear attractive or successful to a supposed viewer, the thing she is not concerned with is her own direct desire. She focuses on sustaining the Other's desire for her. In therapy, the obsessive cannot formulate the words to convey the problem that needs attention. On the other hand, the hysteric is one who knows and overwhelms the analyst with stories from the week. This too is a defense mechanism, unconsciously aiming for repetition.

PERVERSION

> On the basis of the confession we hear from the neurotic or pervert of the ineffable jouissance he finds in losing himself in the fascinating image, we can gauge the power of a hedonism that introduces us to the ambiguous relations between reality and pleasure.[49]

The category of perversion should not be conflated with the term's colloquial usage; the term has no overtly sexual connotation in psychoanalysis but instead implies, as with preceding psychopathological states, a particular relationship between the conscious and unconscious. It is true that perversion may lend itself to non-normative behavior due to the way the conscious-unconscious relationship plays, but perversion also has a higher potential for successfully navigating the big Other's demands. In addition to the conscious-unconscious split, perversion contains a second

49. Lacan, *Écrits*, 222.

split within the ego itself. The split-ego selects a preferred narrative but is at least partially aware of what it disavows.

In his essay on psychoanalysis and criminology, Lacan speculates a close correlation should exist between criminal behavior and perversion even though he cautions this relationship should not be abused to call every criminal a pervert. It is the object-fixations, stagnations of emotional or psychic development, and the relationship of ego to repression that determine whether the label of perversion is appropriate.[50] Freud had less to say on perversion, so its usage is more a product of Lacan's work. It appears to be a category much closer to neurosis than either are to psychosis. Certainly perverts repress just as neurotics do, but the pervert is primarily defined by the mechanism of *fetish disavowal* and his fantasy that he is the object of the big Other's desire.

Like the neuroses, perversion is a cluster of categories, but perversion receives no subcategories in Lacan's work. Fetish disavowal indicates the way in which the pervert selects a fetish-object as a stand-in for what it represses. The disavowed thing cannot be named without inducing severe anxiety. Anyone who has run afoul of a sociopath will understand the basic function and structure of fetish disavowal. Anti-social personality disorder displays highly sociable, friendly behavior until interactions trigger a latent insecurity. The socializing of the sociopath appears genuinely engaged but is in fact only a façade used to gather others into its controlled group. Red flags begin to surface in the sociopath's interactions—variations on narcissistic stories, histories of broken relationships, constant justification of all negative actions, high emphasis on narcissistic uniqueness—but those in the sociopath's circle are usually able to carry on with amiable interactions until they trip a key defense mechanism. There are usually a small cluster of narratives that the sociopath unconsciously uses to maintain his narrative of narcissistic uniqueness, and threatening one of these mechanisms (even quite by accident) will require the sociopath to aggressively cut ties with the offender. Put more simply: the only rule when dealing with a sociopath is to never name the unwritten rule. Naming what is repressed, or disavowed via fetish in the case of the pervert, is the highest of sins.

> In the end the point aimed at by the position of the perverse masochist is the desire to reduce himself to this nothing that is the

---

good, to this thing that is treated like an object, to this slave whom one trades back and forth and whom one shares.[51]

Though perversion is closer to neurosis, it does have its similarities to psychosis as well.[52] Or more accurately, perversion is based on particular instances of delusion that constitute the norm for psychosis. Delusion is perversion at its simplest.[53] Lacan claims sexuality always has a level of perversion inasmuch as it desires the other in a way sustained by object-fantasy.[54] And for all this theoretical progress on the nature of perversion, Lacan jokingly laments that psychoanalysis has yet to invent a novel perversion.[55]

> To return to fantasy, let us say that the pervert imagines he is the Other in order to ensure his own jouissance, and that this is what the neurotic reveals when he imagines he is a pervert—in his case, to ensure control over the Other.[56]

So as the axiom *one's desire is the desire of the Other* functions as a submitting in obsessives and sustaining in hysterics, we could say that the pervert desires to prop up a fantasy of the Other enjoying the pervert. The pervert acquires *jouissance* in a roundabout way by fantasizing the Other as fantasizing about the pervert. Perversion, more than any other psychopathology, desires to *be* the object (cause of) desire for the big Other. The hysteric aims to sustain the desire of the Other, and the case of Dora shows that it does not necessarily matter whether the hysteric is the target of the Other's desire; the Other's desire simply must be maintained for *something*. On the other hand, the pervert only cares to sustain the Other's desire if he himself is the object of desire. Though the hysteric has all the real power, the pervert is the one that fantasizes it has the power, desiring to be the God of the other. The sexual relationship of the pervert to another is sustained by the pervert choosing to believe something about the other's sexual desire that might be totally misaligned with the other's true desires, but the relationship is stable so long as the pervert is able to disavow knowledge of the other's (lack of) enjoyment.

51. Lacan, *Ethics of Psychoanalysis*, 239.
52. Lacan, *Psychoses*, 5.
53. Ibid., 44.
54. Lacan, *Encore*, 86.
55. Lacan, *Ethics of Psychoanalysis*, 15.
56. Lacan, *Écrits*, 699.

Disavowal of reality plays out in every part of the pervert's life. This can certainly be detrimental, but again, disavowal is what allows the pervert to navigate the Other's demands with less anxiety. The pervert desires to be the elusive missing object of another person, the part of life without which their partner cannot live. It is a fundamentally narcissistic relation to reality, rather than submissive (in obsessives) or unsatisfied (in hysterics). Perversion has a "privileged place of jouissance"[57] by having no anxiety at (and actively thriving off of) thinking of itself as the object a of the big Other. I previously extended Scheber's imaginary fantasy as $(a \diamond A)$. Though the perverse fundamental fantasy is still that of a split-subject desiring an object $(\$ \diamond a)$, we could say that he imagines his fantasy as $(a \diamond A)$. He "makes himself the instrument of the Other's jouissance."[58] The perverse desire is a defense, for perversion requires the fantasy of a limit.[59]

TRANSFERENCE

One singularly important concept for Lacanian analysis is the topic of transference. I have postponed its discussion until we could explore it in relation to psychopathology. Transference involves an analyzed subject exporting or projecting a part of herself onto the analyst. It may come in the form of trust, and it may come in the form of anger. The analyst must wait until the patient erupts at the analyst (signifying that the analyst's opinion is getting under the analysand's skin) before knowing that the interpretation will be taken seriously by the analysand. Similarly, the analysand that lies to the analyst can only be helped once she cares enough to feel the weight of her self-deceptive narratives. Until the moment of transference, which may and likely will happen many times over the course of analysis, the sessions are biding their time. For the analyst to speak her interpretation before the point of transference is to speak too soon.[60] It matters not whether the pre-transference interpretation is wrong or right; too soon is wrong regardless. Indeed, sometimes we know the truth and, equally, know it is not yet the moment to speak it.

---

57. Ibid., 697.
58. Ibid.
59. Ibid., 699.
60. Lacan, *Four Fundamental Concepts of Psychoanalysis*, 130.

> The analyst's interpretation merely reflects the fact that the uncon-
> scious . . . has already in its formations—dreams, slips of tongue
> or pen, witticisms or symptoms—proceeded by interpretations.
> The Other, the capital Other, is already there in every opening,
> however fleeting it may be, of the unconscious.[61]

Fink describes it as a "transfer of affect (evoked in the past by people and events) into the here and now of the analytic setting."[62] Transference happens between the analysand and analyst, but it has nothing to do with the analyst. The analyst is only the canvas upon which the analysand paints her anger, bringing the repressed out into the open so that aggression can be analyzed rationally in the third person. But it is important to understand this only works because the analysand *resists the Real*. She resists formulating her trauma and instead keeps it operative in the unconscious. What is repressed always returns, e.g., an angry outburst that has nothing to do with the analyst it is directed toward, and transference brings the repressed out into the clinical setting by triggering unconscious defenses or resistance. What is unconscious becomes acted out, and the clinic is the stage.

Freud discovered transference in the case of Anna O., a hysterical neurotic whose sessions were going nowhere in spite of an over-abundance of stories handed to the analyst. Her stories covered everything in her life except sexuality, and they apparently had very little to do with any true conflict causing any need for therapy in the first place. Lacan refers to this scatter-shot overload of stories as "the chimney-sweeping treatment."[63] When her analyst suggested that her sexless stories must mean she is quite preoccupied with sexuality, she became enraged. Lacan's theory of metonymy says the signifier always points to something else, creating a signifying chain that becomes something more than the sum of its parts. The hermeneutics of interpretation require that the subject be invested enough to dislodge the signifiers, thereby breaking with the false narrative she tells herself.

> Now, what is hermeneutics, if it is not to read, in the succession of
> man's mutations, the progress of the signs according to which he
> constitutes his history, the progress of his history—a history that
> may also, at the fringes, extend into less definite times?[64]

61. Ibid.

62. Fink, *Clinical Introduction to Lacanian Psychoanalysis*, 40.

63. Lacan, *Four Fundamental Concepts of Psychoanalysis*, 157.

64. Ibid., 153.

Transference closes a door to self-deception, and interpretation becomes a decisive act, "for it is to the beauty one must speak."[65] The subject-supposed-to-know—normally meaning the analyst but just as equally meaning the colleague, parent, friend, or person of authority with which we speak—is merely there, so far as transference is concerned, to be the screen for projection.

> As soon as the subject who is supposed to know exists somewhere
> ... there is transference.[66]

Lacan's concept of transference allows us to think of analysis as a double loop, in which the analysand initially goes around the outer circle by demanding help from the analyst. Analysis continues to go around in circles until a precise moment when the analysand spirals inward, that is to say, nothing can be done to help until the analysand's unconscious desires are evoked to the point of transference. Transference occurs at the moment projection upon the analyst confronts the analysand with her own unconscious motivations she has concealed from herself. Once the line of "identification" (of the analysand's unconscious with the analyst, who takes the place of the big Other for the analysand) has been breached, the analyst can affiliate with the healthy part of the subject's conscious ego,[67] and they can explore the analysand's unconscious together. Transference exposes the difference with the demands and injunctions of the big Other and the subject's actual drives, so the analyst must guide the analysand as she learns to reformulate what she desires.[68] After the interior loop of transference and resumption is complete, when the big Other loses operative power for the analysand (at least, the particular problem from the big Other that brought the analysand to the therapy this time), the analysand is able to reorient her what she desires without the injunctions and judgments of the big Other.

TRAVERSING THE FUNDAMENTAL FANTASY

The analyst approaches psychosis, neurosis, and perversion with separate methods to produce the best result for each disposition. Fink describes the foci of analysis as such: the psychotic needs alienation, the pervert needs

65. Ibid., 131.
66. Ibid., 232.
67. Ibid., 130.
68. Ibid., 273.

separation, and the neurotic needs to traverse the fundamental fantasy.[69] After successful transference, we begin to *traverse the fantasy* and reformulate our pathological fantasies as a healthy drive.[70] We discussed the over-identification strategy, which allowing the absurdities of an imagined (though not lived) ideology. Playing as if one truly believes the rhetoric, acting *as-if*, corrodes an ideology by exposing its underside. This strategy traverses the fantasies of the ideology and takes them to their conclusion, which allows the ideology to self-destruct under its own unbearable demands. Lefort's case study of the child Robert in the first chapter succeeded by allowing the child to play out his aggression against his mother by misdirecting it at his analyst. Robert traversed a fantasy that could not be acted out on the absent mother, but it was enough to begin normal development.

I described the neurotic as matheme ($\$\diamondsuit a$), designating a Subject split into conscious and unconscious in relation to an imaginary object (cause of) desire. This is a fantasy, and if we were to expand this matheme to account for how the neurotic actually lives, we could write it as ($\$\diamondsuit a\lozenge\!\!\!\!/\,A$).[71] In this expanded matheme, I am describing two relationships, the left half being the relationship between the subject and the desired object and the right half showing the relationship between the desired object and its source in the big Other. The strikethrough over the relationship between a and A designates the analysand's ignorance of the source of her desire. She believes she desires what she chooses, but no matter what she desires, she is actually desiring what the big Other has told her to desire. Neurotics, obsessives and hysterics alike, remain oblivious to their conditioning by the big Other, preferring to chase objects rather than do the hard work of uncovering why this object should be desired in the first place. On my account of the expanded matheme, it is also worth noting that the ignored right half is the delusional's false-fantasy, whether psychotic or perverse, written as ($a\diamondsuit A$). By writing the matheme in this way, I am suggesting the neurotic represses knowledge of delusion, which is what constitutes moments of perversion and the entirety of psychosis.

Further, what the expanded matheme should suggest is that we are never simply one psychopathology or the other. One needs a great deal of

69. Fink, *Clinical Introduction to Lacanian Psychoanalysis*, 195.

70. Lacan, *Four Fundamental Concepts of Psychoanalysis*, 273.

71. I should clarify this expanded matheme is my creation, not Lacan's. Of the fantasy mathemes I use throughout this book, the representation for fundamental fantasy is the only one directly from Lacan. Mathemes diverging from his basic formula are my interpretation.

delusion in order to be a stable neurotic. We are primarily oriented for one category but are never exclusively such. Neurosis always has an element of perversion and vice versa, and both are at risk for psychosis. As the next chapter will explore, we may have a tendency (especially with obsessives) to adopt the language and modes of thought from another psychopathology when our defense mechanisms are overwhelmed with anxiety.

> After the mapping of the subject in relation to the *a*, the experi-
> ence of the fundamental fantasy becomes the drive. What, then,
> does he who has passed through the experience of this opaque
> relation to the origin, to the drive, become? How can a subject who
> has traversed the radical fantasy experience the drive? This is the
> beyond of analysis, and has never been approached.[72]

We are never simply "cured." Our desires, symptoms, and beliefs can reorient, but we are always tossed by the whims of the Symbolic. Thus far in this book, I have equated the object (cause of) desire and the beliefs we desire to believe in. My equating the two has been a bit of short-hand in the interest of applying this material to theology. It would be more accurate to say that a belief is an retroactive affect of the desired object which is in turn directed by the drives of the big Other. The aim of a drive is to endlessly encircle the object it aims at rather than directly acquiring it; we acquire more satisfaction (*jouissance*) by getting just close enough to our goal to never notice we are engaging in repetition. Beliefs are Imaginary. They are the way we justify our condition.

The question naturally arose as to whether a good psychoanalyst ought to be an atheist. Further, could one consider analysis complete if one still needed belief in a god? It is a question of little importance to Lacan, who replied, "I'll tell you that, regardless of what an obsessional bears out in his words, if he hasn't been divested of his obsessional structure, you can be sure that, as an obsessional, he believes in God."[73] If the analysand still demands direction from the analyst, the analysand effectively believes in God, that is to say, the representative of the big Other has merely shifted from one to another. The more peculiar point is that those who think of themselves as true believers sustain their belief by unconscious unbelief, "because if they did believe, it would be visible. If they did believe as strongly as all that,

---

72. Lacan, *Four Fundamental Concepts of Psychoanalysis*, 273.
73. Lacan, *Anxiety*, 308.

the consequences of that belief wouldn't go unnoticed, when in actual fact this belief remains strictly invisible."[74]

> This is the true dimension of atheism. The atheist would be he who has succeeded in doing away with the fantasy of the Almighty.[75]

With the importance we place on a particular belief we signify one of two things. On the one hand, a true belief has the structure of a fiction[76] and is an effective way for the subject to cover over the irreducible gaps and inconsistencies resulting from repression. Legitimate belief, and by that I mean beliefs that are natural to a person's psychopathological orientation, may not be true in the sense of factual accuracy, but it is an effective Imaginary conception produced from a (hopefully) relatively healthy Symbolic network.

> The fictitious is not, in effect, in its essence that which deceives, but is precisely what I call the symbolic.[77]

On the other hand, there are beliefs we adopt from communal pressure. These can be entirely healthy and necessary for tribal cohesion. We simply must adopt certain fictions in order to operate in a society of fictions, and we have not the time to analyze each belief with the scrutiny needed to return some sort of universalized, absolute veracity. This repression via fiction allows us to live in community. But we have likely all had the experience of wanting to cease believing in something we cannot seem to leave behind. We fear the disdain of or expulsion from the community. The disgust we feel at a particular belief causes anxiety, but perhaps the belief-anxiety does surpass the threshold of anxiety caused by leaving the community. The calculus of costs will change over time, but people have a remarkable ability to remain in communities that express beliefs foreign to their unconscious. The neurotic state ($\$\diamond a \diamond A$) is precarious. So what happens when a person with one psychopathology is pressured to adopt the beliefs and demands of another? And just as a group in which every personality is kind and perfectly amiable can nevertheless produce hostility as a community, what happens when a group of neurotics foolishly produce and reward ideologies of cynicism?

74. Ibid.
75. Ibid.
76. Lacan, *Ethics of Psychoanalysis*, 12.
77. Lacan, *Four Fundamental Concepts of Psychoanalysis*, 12.

Chapter 5

The Fool and the Knave

In various places people are surprised. What's eating them, these students, the little dears, our favorites, the darlings of civilization? What's up with them? Those who are saying this are playing the fool, this is what they are paid to do.[1]

All I can do is tell the truth. No, that isn't so—I have missed it. There is no truth that, in passing through awareness, does not lie. But one runs after it all the same.[2]

THERE WAS AN ATHENIAN statesman named Phocion who, when rousingly applauded at the end of his speech, turned aside dejected and asked what he said that must have been so foolish.[3] There is another joke Freud loved where a pauper begged money from a wealthy baron who was happy to oblige with a sum large enough to stretch a few weeks. Later that same day, the benefactor entered a restaurant and was angered upon seeing the beggar enjoying a delicacy of salmon mayonnaise. He wasted no time reproaching the beggar for such a waste of money, to which the beggar excitedly replied, "I don't understand—if I haven't any money I *can't* eat salmon mayonnaise, and if I have money I *mustn't* eat salmon mayonnaise. Well, then, when *am* I to eat salmon mayonnaise?"[4]

1. Lacan, *Other Side of Psychoanalysis*, 164.
2. Lacan, *Four Fundamental Concepts of Psychoanalysis*, vii.
3. Freud, *Jokes and Their Relation to the Unconscious*, 59.
4. Ibid., 50.

The story could easily critique our reluctance to donate on the grounds that funding will be misused. Neither is it difficult to use this joke to critique ways in which society decides certain classes do not deserve the luxuries another class enjoys. These are easy connections to make, but what makes for a joke is that the beggar played the fool and in so doing exposed the hypocrisy of the wealthy baron. The benefactor did not believe the beggar to be an equal human peer, but instead the beggar served as a way for the baron to pay for his guilt. The baron's hypocrisy was only exposed by the beggar's full immersion within the baron's lifestyle, the beggar acting foolishly as if he really believed he was an equal.

Nietzsche condemned those who "served the people and the superstition of the people, all you famous wise men—and *not* truth. And that is precisely why you were accorded respect. And that is also why your lack of faith was tolerated: it was a joke and a circuitous route to the people."[5] A similar logic works in nearly every story we have for the erratic philosopher Diogenes the Cynic. Once, when Alexander the Great stood and gazed down at the homeless Diogenes sunning himself on the street, the emperor asked if there was anything he could do for him. Not a respecter of position, Diogenes asked the emperor if he could stop blocking the sun.[6] Upon seeing a man dressed in a most expensive and elaborate manner, Diogenes mocked him, "If it's for men, you're a fool; if for woman, a knave."[7] When someone asked why those who give to beggars never show such charity to philosophers, Diogenes replied, "Because they think they may one day be lame or blind but never expect to become philosophers."[8]

Plato, who referred to Diogenes as "Socrates gone mad," once reproached the cynic for his chosen poverty. If he could only learn to please the god Dionysus, Plato told him, he would not have to scrape by on vegetables. Diogenes replied that if Plato could learn to be subsist on vegetables then he would never again need to please the gods.[9] Every story is one of over-identifying with the unconscious logic of his interlocutor. His logic was cynical but his language was foolish—he was far to clever to believe most of what he said, but he demonstrated the way in which foolishness

---

5. Nietzsche, "Thus Spoke Zarathustra," 214.

6. Dobbin, *Cynic Philosophers from Diogenes to Julian*, 31.

7. Laertius, *Lives of the Philosophers*, 143.

8. Ibid., 144.

9. Dobbin, *Cynic Philosophers from Diogenes to Julian*, 34.

and cynicism support each other on the provisional condition that neither are chased to their rational conclusion.

Early on in his career, Lacan was ever skeptical about deploying psychoanalysis against group dynamics, imploring his colleagues, "We must rigorously distinguish psychoanalytic theory from the ever renewed fallacious attempts to base notions such as 'modal personality,' 'national character,' or 'collective superego' on analytic theory."[10] The fear was justified, for if psychoanalysis sought to avoid digression into subjective mysticism verging on the religious, it needed to maintain its status as a science. Yet psychoanalysis became such a powerfully popular avenue within critical theory, making sense of politics where little else is able to shed light on the vicissitudes, paradoxes, mixed interests, and outright lies of our modern political economy. To be clear, Lacan was no political theorist and was deeply pessimistic about the possibilities for political reform. He was even more clear with regard to Freud, whom he considered in no way a progressive political theorist.[11] But there is a turn in the seventh seminar on ethics that continues in the seventeenth seminar on politics, and it is this turn that the remainder of the this book will build on. Communities have their own psychopathology that is more than the sum of its individuals, and it is my wager that the same communal psychopathology that grounds Žižek's political work can be found in our religious communities. In this chapter, we shall put Christianity itself on the psychoanalyst's couch, interrogating her vicissitudes and repetitions. We are first confronted with the figures of the left-wing fool and the right-wing knave.

LEFT-WING FOOLS

> The "fool" is an innocent, a simpleton, but truths issue from his mouth that are not simply tolerated but adopted, by virtue of the fact that this "fool" is sometimes clothed in the insignia of the jester.[12]

Progressives strive toward goals whose attainment is ever-postponed. The liberal politician's rhetoric is not unlike the "chimney sweeping" strategy of the hysterical neurotic. The analysand stirs up a great deal of soot, but the stories with which the analysand overloads the analyst have a logic

10. Lacan, *Écrits*, 108.

11. Lacan, *Ethics of Psychoanalysis*, 183.

12. Ibid., 182.

of misdirection. If the chimney sweeping is successful, the misdirected analyst will misdiagnose the symptomatic behavior and may even praise the analysand for apparent progress. The analyst must remain rigorous with such analysands, which is not at all to say the analysand is aware of the misdirection conducted. The unconscious desire for unhealth sustains the conscious presumption of health. If the injunction of the unconscious is repetition, the analyst must assume resistance is in play in each session whether apparent or otherwise. Fink goes so far as to advise his students to interpret requests for breaks or appointment cancellations due to health or death in the family as resistance mechanisms. Ultimately the analyst cannot know which excuse is legitimate, so she must default to the assumption that wherever there is a narrative, there is resistance.

Lacan operated in a mid-century Parisian culture with a radicalized left, and though America does not have a leftist party, his observations map well enough onto the liberal party. We can think of the left-right spectrum as two parallel axes, one of freedom-restriction of personal rights and another of another of noncapitalist-capitalist economics.[13] For those who take the left-right spectrum to be useful, this traditionally places liberalism in the center. Liberalism exists only in a democracy, and the liberal party must convince citizens to cast votes by isolating and exploiting narcissistic-cathexis. It must use its voters' attachments via chimney sweeping rhetoric. It matters not whether the issue we identify with is the environment, the rights of minorities, or the plight of the poor; all that matters to the leader is that we latch onto at least one cause. We cast our votes, and the party retains its paradoxes and inconsistencies, its mixed motives and conflicting drives. It counts on citizens never noticing the repetition, never noticing that so little has been done for the cause to which they attached.

> When today's Left bombards the capitalist system with demands that it obviously cannot fulfill (Full employment! Retain the welfare state! Full rights for immigrants!), it is basically playing a game of hysterical provocation, of addressing the Master with a demand that will be impossible for him to meet, and will thus expose his impotence.[14]

The fool believes in a direct and naïve fashion. And progressives, whether of the liberal or leftist variety, do indeed seem to believe directly in their causes. Foolishness is not used here in the negative sense but in the

13. I highly recommend Crockett, *Radical Political Theology*.
14. Žižek, *Puppet and the Dwarf*, 43.

sense of direct belief or honesty. We should hope for a world in which fool-ishly direct belief can be assumed, but sans that counterfactual reality, we learn to read hidden motives. The progressive may be on the winning side of history on any number of social issues while falling for its own resistance narrative that diagnoses the symptom instead of the disease.

Is this not exactly the frustration we have with the liberal pundit mocking the supposed foolishness of the extremist politician? The posi-tion of the liberal pundit during an interview with an extremist is usually a choice between (1) insulting the guest's position by exposing the disturbing conclusion of a line of thought or (2) countering, in a manner ironically recalling William F. Buckley's famous refrain, "I will not insult your in-telligence by suggesting you really believe what you just said." Detailing inconsistencies immediately devolves into a "gotcha" campaign, leaving the viewer unsure now of whether the liberal pundit believes what was just said about what the politician supposedly believes. Whereas the conservative pundit has an expected party line, the position of the liberal is always un-sure. As viewers we intuitively understand the language game signaling to the respective sides, but the liberal pundit perfectly displays this (ultimately quite anxious) desire to believe in the direct sense.

The hysteric desires to play out an act with the analyst, distracting just enough so that the symptom cannot be named, the repetition can remain veiled, and life can go on with only the most basic and irrelevant details changed. The liberal intellectual desires exactly the same, hoping the voter-analyst can be deceived. Lacan jeered at his protesting students: "A certain number of biases are your daily fare and limit the import of your insurrec-tions to the shortest term, to the term, quite precisely, that gives you no discomfort—they certainly don't change your world view, for that remains perfectly spherical. The signified finds its center wherever you take it."[15] Just enough will be changed so that things basically remain the same, and we will cheer.

RIGHT-WING KNAVES

The ideology of the right-wing intellectual, is precisely to play the role of what he is in fact, namely, a "knave." In other words, he

---

15. Lacan, *Encore*, 42.

doesn't retreat from the consequences of what is, called realism; that is, when required, he admits he's a crook.[16]

On the other hand, the knave knows the farce. The knave is a cynic in the purest sense of the term. Not every cynic is a knave, but every knave is a cynic. The jaded cynic begins by casting doubt upon the motives of others, but the path concludes when we no longer care for how we justify the acquisition of our goal. Cynicism is not a simply realism and not necessarily negative, but instead it is only immediately interested in the ends rather than the means. The manipulative knave lies when inevitably required, but the citizenry already accounts for this. "All politicians lie" becomes a normalized justification for complacency among those who cannot perceive the differences before their eyes and vie instead for moderation. It is what we tell ourselves and even begin to believe so that we never realize there are both quantitative *and* qualitative differences between the strategies deployed within different political ideologies. There are those who so deeply desire to hear what their naïvely populist ears want to hear that they never detect the dubious, but there are also those in the know who align with the knave because the fetishized ends always justify the means. Many know the knave is not foolish enough to believe what he is saying, but they give their votes all the same.

The casual dismissal of the political lie has a double-effect of complicity and repression. First, is it not odd that a population accepts the lying leader? Second, is it not true that while "all politicians lie," in reality it is only the politicians of the opposing party that we truly think of as liars? The statement of doubt is a fleetingly conscious cover for the unconscious nonrecognition of a serious flaw, but those lukewarm persons who occasionally acknowledge politicians lie are awarded a socially prized position of faux-impartiality. There is an old joke that says there is nobody more dishonest than a priest who is paid to lie to the parishioner, but the remark is nothing more than a fetish disavowal that allows parishioner to continue acting as if she believed in the priest's direct honesty. As Heschel wrote, "Neutrality is an illusion. At the end of his days man always emerges either as a priest or as a pirate . . . The primary task, therefore, is not how to deal with the evil, but *how to deal with neutral.*"[17] We cannot afford to be moderate; impartiality is for those without eyes to see.

16. Lacan, *Ethics of Psychoanalysis*, 183.

17. Heschel, *God In Search of Man*, 382–83.

The right-wing leader has the education and experience to know that much of what he needs to say to win the hearts of a demographic will be purely foolish. Take the extreme example of fascism, an abused word with a rather simple meaning, namely, the perfect union of capital interests and the state. Fascism, like liberalism, exists in a democracy and requires the support of the people. The obstacle it faces is the simple matter that capitalism's defining profit reallocation does not work out well for the vast majority. Capitalism thrives when its population lacks the understanding of a system that, by definition, cannot ever pay its workers for the value they contribute to their corporations; if we are paid for *all* the value we contribute, it is by definition not a specifically capitalist enterprise. Economic crises, wealth inequality, and even lack of basic necessities are not accidents of this arrangement but are instead predictable and required sacrifices. Thus the fascist, in order to capture the support of a population whose lifestyle is directly threatened by moneyed interests, must deploy the perverse strategy of fetish disavowal.

The figure of the Jew became the standard exclusionary device in the West, but modern forms of fascism in Europe and North America deploy the same basic structure by blaming the immigrant, the ethnic or sexual minority, education and science, etc. Max Horkheimer and Theodor W. Adorno, who are interesting to read as intellectuals processing anti-Semitism during the war, describe the phenomenon as a repressed mimesis. "Anti-Semitism is based on a false projection. It is the counterpart of true mimesis, and fundamentally related to the repressed form; in fact, it is probably the morbid expression of repressed mimesis. Mimesis imitates the environment, but false projection makes the environment like itself."[18] Psychoanalysis views anti-Semitism (and xenophobia in general) as a case of morbid projection where the subject's own unconscious taboo impulses are transferred upon an external object.[19] The exclusion of the object (whether in sacrificial or murderous form) reveals some truth about the subject. They continue, "But in Fascism this behavior is made political; the object of the illness is deemed true to reality; and the mad system becomes the reasonable norm in the world and deviation from it a neurosis."[20] The consequences between extremist exclusion in the 1940s and today clearly have vast differences, but the structure of exclusion—for the purposes of

18. Horkheimer and Adorno, *Dialectic of Enlightenment*, 178.

19. Ibid., 192.

20. Ibid., 178.

projection and distraction—remains the same. Also remaining the same is the fact that the leader on the far right does not need to believe what he says in order for his rhetoric to function.

There is an important distinction we must always make between foolish speech and direct belief in foolishness, and much of our political debate corresponds to a confusion over whether to interpret speech as a staged act or an honest position. We see an excellent example of this distinction in the birther conspiracies directed against Barack Obama. Surveys on the prevalence of public belief have consistently shown between two-thirds and three-quarters Republicans (as well as a not-insignificant number of Democrats) agreeing Obama is "definitely" or "possibly" foreign born. At no point has any survey shown even half of the opposition party willing to say the president is a US citizen. Even if these views are seldom expressed in public, surveys consistently suggest they are rampant. We would be mistaken if we presumed all those espousing these views directly believed in the conspiracy. The men and women in party leadership are highly educated members of society, but they had to court a population for whom this exclusionary belief had been cultivated as a master-signifier. Because one reaps what one sows, the politicians benefiting from the cultivation of this conspiracy immediately must also distance themselves so as not to appear delusional or unnecessarily partisan in the eyes of independents.

I do not at all mean to defend birtherism as anything less than outright xenophobia, but media consistently treats the conspiracy theories as either (1) unpopular fringe beliefs or (2) inexplicable, mass delusion. However, the truth is that the delusional affirmation became a master signifier for the tribe, and master signifiers are always doing something different from what they literally affirm. Psychoanalytic metonymy intrinsically assumes signifiers, even delusional ones, always signify something else. In this case, to question the conspiracy was to blaspheme the Holy Spirit of the party, signaling the politician was not "one of us." Thus as his poll numbers failed to catch up, the educated and adept GOP nominee delivered a joke shortly before the 2012 election—nobody has ever questioned my citizenship— that clearly signified tribal affiliation rather than direct belief. An ideology can sustain limitless internal contradictions so long as the metonymy of the whole provides a coherent identity.

COLLECTIVE FOOLISHNESS AND THE RISE OF THE KNAVE

The "foolery" which constitutes the individual style of the left-wing intellectual gives rise to a collective "knavery."[21]

Lacan wagers that collective foolishness gives rise to ideologies of knavery. And though he does not say it outright, we might also guess the inverse: collectives of knavish leaders attract foolish crowds. This could partially account for rightward drift in politics over time, but it certainly accounts for the figure of the cynic that so often leads the political or religious community. The knave may be an obsessive or hysteric outside the job, but the office of leadership requires adopting a perverse desire to be the object of desire for the big Other. I have previously reduced the pervert to the desire to be the God of the other (or to narcissistically desire himself through the Gaze of the Other), and we should understand that whenever a pervert and a neurotic interact, there is a differential in relationship compatibility. A relationship between the pervert and the neurotic will almost certainly lose Symbolic balance, and it is the neurotic that will chiefly suffer. In the same way, neurotic communities that desire to believe in the direct sense of foolish honesty will tend to suffer under the pressure of a knavish ideological model. I do not mean this absolutely; it could very well be the case that the split-ego of perversion is exactly what a community needs. Žižek argues convincingly that Christian theology is inherently perverse and is at its best when it embraces its posture of half-belief.[22] I tend to agree with the caveat that this is only healthy when the community desires to understand the actual nature and purposes of its ideology and leadership. Unfortunately this is seldom the case, for religion is usually far more adept at providing security than truth.

It need not be the case that the leader (as an individual) is a pervert or cynical knave—I do not at all mean to say that clerics and politicians are necessarily perverse knaves. I mean instead to say there is a certain trajectory that needs our attention: we desire a (leader)-supposed-to-know to stand in for the all-knowing big Other, and this dependent need produces a social pressure for deception. The leader might be an honest figure who succumbs to the pressure of a cynical ideology. On the one hand, it could be the case that every single person in a community is a foolishly, honestly

21. Lacan, *Ethics of Psychoanalysis*, 183.
22. See Žižek, *Puppet and the Dwarf.*

direct participant while still manifesting a cynical ideology as a collective. But on the other hand, we have an inherent desire for a leader that "knows," and the leader that brandishes certainly is more likely to be a cynic than a fool. The foolish masses desire a knave, the knave desires to lead a fool, and the knave is the one who will benefit from the arrangement.

While Lacan claims groups of fools produce leaders who are knaves, he does not explicitly state the obverse, namely, that groups of cynics or knaves produce leaders who are fools. I do not think it much a stretch to presume this would be the case. We see especially in American liberalism a desire to be connected and knowledgeable on the issues, and yet it can only manage to produce leaders that play the part of a weak fool rather than a radical progressive. The problem is more confounding in religion. Everyone desires a leader who believes in their message, but we understand the cleric has all the same doubts as anyone else. The more dogmatic the belief system and associated behaviors, the more the cleric must repress, which in turn leads to deception, indiscretions, and even criminal transgression. Dogmatism produces the knave. On the other side of the spectrum, religious groups with low levels of dogmatism attract those who intuitively understand the language games in play yet prefer clerics who will act as if they believe with all the certainty of the knave, if perhaps in a more believable fashion. The point in either case is the cleric must occupy an oddly inverse position from the parishioner collective, and to misunderstand the inverted uses of the parishioner-cleric systems leads to conflict.

I claim that we see this general pattern in religious communities: *perversion pressures neurosis to reorient as obsessionalism via hysteric and/or psychotic language.* The choice of hysteric or psychotic language is arbitrary and depends on the inclinations of the group, but the generally neurotic community tends to reward leaders or ideologies of knaves. The cynical leader able to co-opt the submissive tendencies of the neurotic public will experience remarkable success in building the collective, but the collective will begin to manifest problems based in inter-psychopathological difference that it will continuously mislabel as a merely a difference of opinions.

BUKHARIN AND KAFKA

Belief is a notion that displays the deadlock characteristic of the Real: on the one hand, nobody can fully assume belief in the first person singular . . . On the other hand, however, no one really escapes belief—a feature that deserves to be emphasized especially today, in our allegedly godless times.[23]

Žižek found a perfect example of this pattern in the story of Nicolay Invanovich Bukharin, a Soviet Central Committee member who had the unfortunate experience of being a district secretary during the Stalinist purges. Bukharin was an intellectual and a true believer in the grand historical cause, serving faithfully for years. He doubtlessly witnessed more than a few red flags encroaching upon the normal order of his community. In religious communities today, these red flags appear as peculiarly grotesque or exclusionary beliefs positioning themselves as orthodoxy's master signifiers rather than hints of communal dysfunction. The symptomatic belief is universalized to represent the whole. To chip away at the symptom sets off anxiety at the prospect of network collapse. There are a number of ways to mitigate this anxiety, but the most common defense mechanism is to disavow anxiety altogether by promoting a belief as fetish. This always puts the community in a continuous personality crisis, unsure whether the creed is repeated in sincerity or cynicism, because "one can never be sure if a positive feature really is what it pretends to be: what if someone merely *pretends* to follow the Party line faithfully in order to conceal his true counter-revolutionary attitude?"[24]

The Kafkaesque show trial under during the purge produced the unofficial motto of the Stalinist era, "The more you are innocent, the more you deserve to be shot." To sin against the Party was one thing, but to say the Party incompetently brought false charges was an unforgivable blasphemy of the Holy Spirit. In Kafka's *The Trial*, the hapless protagonist Josef K. faces redacted charges under a secret court whose jurisdiction and procedures are perpetually concealed. Josef K.'s only break comes in the form of an elderly lawyer who agrees to represent him and assures K. the trials do not always result in conviction. The catch is that the trials do not end without convictions either. The only hope is to prolong the bureaucratic process, to go on about one's life as normally as possible, and to die a natural death before the court declares its inevitable verdict. The process wears on Josef K.'s spirit, creating a reluctantly submissive drone who appears to be the only person entirely unsurprised by the plot's abrupt conclusion.

23. Žižek, *Did Somebody Say Totalitarianism?*, 88.
24. Ibid., 100.

> Religious people thus confer upon truth the status of guilt . . .
> Truth in religion is relegated to so-called "eschatological" ends,
> which is to say that truth appears only as final cause, in the sense
> that it is deferred to an end-of-the-world judgment.[25]

Bukharin ran afoul of the party over the violent collectivization of farms. The transcript of the trial shows the sincere foolishness of believing he could best serve the Party by playing the role of the court jester rather than sparing them the trouble by suicide. To this, they could only laugh, and Bukharin retorted, "Look, if I am a saboteur, a son of a bitch, then why spare me? I make no claims to anything. I am just describing what's on my mind, what I am going through. If this in any way entails any political damage, however minute, then no question about it, I'll do whatever you say. (Laughter.) Why are you laughing? There is absolutely nothing funny about any of this."[26]

The knave is not threatened by foolishness, however sincere and perceptive it may be. On the contrary, the knave depends on reactionary disagreement. Bukharin confessed to many political sins in the early 1930s but maintained his innocence of treason until his demise in 1938. The sin for which he would not confess was not quite what he was tried for; the show trial was indeed about the relatively normalized (though still capital) offense of treason, but the trial began to expose how dependent the Central Committee was on the ritual of false confession. The point of a show trial is not to discover truth but to follow a pattern that sustains the dominant ideology. By professing innocence, he exposed the ritual as farce, nothing more than a formal and empty gesture.

The show trial put on fool display the antagonism between a foolish neurotic Committee member and a Party that had evolved to a state of full perversion. The perverse fantasy sees itself as the object of the big Other; whatever questions this status of the Other's *sole* object of desire must be disavowed. On the other hand, Bukharin was a neurotic who falsely imagined he and Stalin were playing the same game of foolishly direct belief in a grand cause, and his fundamental fantasy ($\$ \lozenge a$) attached to an object of desire that Stalin could fill as a substitute (though he would never truly exist as the object Bukharin sought).

Bukharin wrote a series of letters from the gulag detailing his desire for Stalin to execute him. He acknowledged the need to sacrifice the man

25. Lacan, *Écrits*, 741.

26. Transcript as quoted in Žižek, *Did Somebody Say Totalitarianism?*, 103.

for the for the sake of the Party and told Stalin the sacrifice of one's friends was a decision any good Bolshevik must be willing to make. He nevertheless continued to fail to recognize the importance of the empty gesture, writing in his final letter to Stalin, "Oh, Lord, if only there were some device which would have made it possible for you to see my soul flayed and ripped open! . . . I ask you one final time for your forgiveness (only in your heart, not otherwise). For that reason I embrace you in my mind. Farewell and remember kindly your wretched N. Bukharin."[27]

When repression collapses and a pre-conscious point of anxiety enters the conscious register, it must be dealt with directly or repressed more deeply again. The split-ego structure of perverse disavow is quite different: anxiety is simply not experienced in the face of conflict (at least, not to the intense degree the neurotic experiences conflict-anxiety) so long as a fetish can stand in for the point of anxiety. This difference can be difficult to diagnose because neurosis and perversion produce identical behavior when in public view. This remains true until the most extreme of anxiety-inducing circumstances wherein the unconscious steps in with brute force to defend the ego from what it does not want to know. Bukharin asked his comrades, whom he considered friends, to admit in secret that the ritual was a farce. The public would never have to know that their leadership did not truly believe in the ritual, but surely—among comrades who had suffered everything together—the purely formal logic of an empty gesture could be acknowledged? "This, precisely, the Party could not grant him," Žižek writes, for "the ritual loses its performative power the moment it is explicitly designated as mere ritual."[28] His fate was the same as seventy-nine of eighty-two district secretaries during the purge.

LUTHER AGAINST ROME

> I am not saying—thought it would not be inconceivable—that the psychoanalytic community is a Church. Yet the question indubitably does arise—what is it in that community that is so reminiscent of religious practice?[29]

Lacan began his seminar on *The Four Fundamental Elements of Psychoanalysis* in the year following his expulsion from the French Psychoanalytic

27. Ibid., 106–7.
28. Žižek, *Did Somebody Say Totalitarianism?*, 109.
29. Lacan, *Four Fundamental Concepts of Psychoanalysis*, 4.

Society, which was not helped by a decade-long feud with the International Psychoanalytic Association. As his increasingly unorthodox ideas enraptured Paris, his more traditional peers grew incensed and began to police the boundaries of their practice. The Gospel, Lacan observed, says that the sign must appear regardless of the tragic fate for its bearer.[30] The new seminar in 1964 at *École Normale Supérieure* explored the four fundamentals of the unconscious, repetition, transference, and the drive. But what makes the turn in his career and thought so interesting is that it could not have come about without the event Lacan himself labels an excommunication.

Martin Luther once asked, "If you will allow people with sensitive feelings to judge, they would consider no person more stinging and unrestrained in his denunciations than Paul. Who is more stinging than the prophets?"[31] He was a clear case of heightened obsessional neurosis if there ever was one. His writings display at once (1) a rigorously rational acumen for mastery of his material and (2) utter exclusion from consciousness the Symbolic elements conditioning his theology. The creative invectives against his disputants, most notable in the exchange of letters with Erasmus, always presumed a lack of rational coherence on the part of the interlocutor rather than a difference of starting assumptions. Luther wrote with the assumption he and his debaters were playing by a similar set of rules and with similar motives. Psychoanalysis locates the subject primarily in the unconscious, thus what makes Luther—and indeed much of confessional theology—difficult to read is the persistent illusion that subjectivity can be controlled and accounted for at the conscious register. Much of his dispute with Rome can be reduced to the mapping of social psychopathology we are exploring in this chapter, and we shall see that Luther matures into his true potential only after coming to terms with differences he and Rome have in motives.

> How does it happen that these good and accommodating men or neighbors . . . let themselves go to the point of falling prey to captivation by the mirages by which their lives, wasting opportunity, allow their essence to escape, by which their passion is toyed with, and by which their being, in the best of cases, only attains the scant reality that is affirmed only insofar as it has never been anything but disappointed?[32]

30. Lacan, *Écrits*, 23.
31. Luther, "Freedom of a Christian," 335.
32. Lacan, *Triumph of Religion*, 7–8.

The Fool and the Knave

Perhaps it is telling that Martin Luder changed his name to Luther, a word derived from the Greek for "freedom." He was born in 1483 to Hans Luder, an unschooled and illiterate copper smelter who made a fairly stable living in Mansfield. Biographers caution against reading too much into his childhood, but discipline of the home was stern with stories including beatings severe enough to draw blood. Though peasant class, Hans Luder was a respected council representative for the community. Having no interest in his father's business, Luther departed to study at Magdebung at the age of fifteen years. He finished his first baccalaureate in 1502 and his master's degree two years later, the same year of the famed turbulent lightning storm during which a prayer traded his life for monastic devotion. True to his promise, he entered the monastery at Erfurt with uncommon zeal for fasting, confession, and maintaining of vows. This is characteristic of the extreme obsessional, for once the rule is in place it should be carried to its rational conclusion. His new life grafted in new commands from the big Other, and guilt increased. Unless repression can be stabilized to minimize guilt, the neurotic must either (1) continuously heighten repression to account for new dissonance or (2) experience an overwhelming anxiety that cracks one's presumptive ideology and reorients itself. Luther appeared incapable of mitigating anxiety or disassociating his identity from beliefs and hierarch. The strategy of further repression was (for the moment) working.

> As a rule the ordinary pious individual, too, performs a ceremonial without concerning himself with its significance, although priests and scientific investigators may be familiar with the—mostly symbolic—meaning of the ritual. In all believers, however, the motives which impel them to religious practices are unknown to them or are represented in consciousness by others which are advanced in their place.[33]

Let us momentarily return to the idea that anxiety is felt precisely when the subject realizes there is no barrier to *jouissance*. Anxiety triggers doubt, the latter being an experience the subject has no control over. In his essay "Obsessive Actions and Religious Practices," Freud argued that people naturally prefer guilt to anxiety, that is to say, we prefer to instate prohibitions and punish ourselves for transgressions in order to maintain repetition. Obsessive-compulsive ceremonials are carried out in private and normally have a primary reason or excuse in the subject's mind. Of course, the compulsive ceremonial will undoubtedly result from alternative

33. Freud, "Obsessive Actions and Religious Practices," 433.

traumas afflicting the unconscious. Religious services and practices bring the private ceremonial out into the open, and though most are able to carry on by ascribing any number of meanings to the ritualistic act, there are those who interrogate the ritual until its meaning breaks down. At the point of anxiety and doubt, the subject has only two options: guilt and repetition or transgressive reconsideration.

Luther's confessor Johann von Staupitz attempted to intervene with some success and suggested such extreme fasting was terrible for his health. He reentered the university at Wittenberg and acquired another series of degrees culminating with his doctorate in 1512. Around this time, Luther traveled to Rome and later recounted his travel as a traumatic exposure to the luxuries, prostitution, the bastard children of cardinals, the licentiousness that he could only repress for a few more years. He was confronted with a duplicitous Curia and a pope who seemed unconcerned with rampant hypocrisy.

> One remains true to [orthodoxy] because one has nothing to say about the doctrine itself.[34]

Of all the things Luther could have picked a fight over, the 95 *Theses* against Tetzel's indulgence campaign was a curious choice. The epiphany on grace traced from his teaching the New Testament between 1512 and 1517, but we could imagine everything from his monastic experience of guilt, disgust at Rome's duplicity, and his pastoral care for the impoverished and illiterate peasants of his parish contributed to selecting the indulgence controversy as the point on which to start the debate. Still, when reading them one has the sense Luther was choosing to ignore the reasons involving money and choosing to treat indulgences as a legitimately theological matter. But after posting the theses on the Wittenberg door on October 31, 1517, he found himself embroiled in skirmishes that quickly escalated beyond the confines of theology into the political feuds of the Holy Roman Empire. The nation state was in its birth, and Hegel observed, there can be no political revolution without spiritual reformation.

In statement that could easily pass as Lacanian, Luther told his readers, "We are never lords of our actions but servants."[35] The *Larger Catechism* contained a revealing excursus on hypocrisy and the possible antagonisms Luther felt. It was a case of arguing something that is really about something

34. Lacan, *Écrits*, 205.
35. Luther, "Disputation against Scholastic Theology," 11.

else, and we see this throughout Luther's work. While examining the sixth commandment Luther argued against the idolization of chastity, claiming it was "not possible to remain chaste outside of marriage; for flesh and blood remain flesh and blood, and natural inclinations and stimulations proceed unrestrained and unimpeded, as everyone observes and experiences."[36] He specifically targeted the clerics who took vows no person could keep: "For no one has so little love and inclination for chastity as those who under the guise of great sanctity avoid marriage and either indulge in open and shameless fornication or secretly do even worse—things too evil to mention, as unfortunately has been experienced all too often."[37] This suggests any and all people who take the vow of chastity fit into two and only two categories: (1) shameless hypocrites who break the vow and (2) the envious and lust-ridden sufferers of "incessant ragings of secret passion."[38] My wager is that this was really a tacit admission of his own condition (presumably the latter category). Luther took these vows as a monk, and by all accounts did not break them until his marriage in 1523. Yet while he desired to believe in the direct sense, all around himself he saw those who flaunted their flagrant disregard for the vow in a cynical manner. There were knaves, and there were fools; Luther was beginning to figure out which he had been.

Truth that escapes is always quite happy to throw away the mask concealing it.[39] The best critiques erupt from inside an ideology's framework precisely when they can no longer *not* erupt. Luther's aggressive criticism was much more than mere dismissal of some ideology he believed himself above; instead, he claimed ideology could not contain itself without rupturing via its own antagonisms. He could say this because he new better than anyone—certainly better than the Curia and perhaps better than the pope himself—what it meant to push the ideals of confession, fasting, sexual abstinence, dogma, etc., to their rational conclusion. His claim was not that he did not believe but that Rome did not believe.

Luther thought of subjectivity as an ego with an opposition of an inner field (faith-unfaith) layered upon an outer opposition (love-wickedness).[40] The creature of faith is able to overcome sin by aligning her will with the

36. Luther, "Large Catechism," 415.

37. Ibid., 415.

38. Ibid.

39. Lacan, *Écrits*, 224.

40. I wish to credit Ingolf Dalferth, whose 2013 lectures at Claremont Graduate University on Luther's concept of subjectivity shaped this section.

will of God, and in this sense God functions as a reality principle taming the pleasure principle. The sinful impulses of the id can be counteracted by the decision-making of the ego provided the ego affiliates with God. This of course cannot be defended by a psychoanalytic perspective that locates subjectivity primarily in the unconscious, but it is interesting that both Luther and Lacan (albeit in very different ways) located all the power in the hands of the big Other. Luther wrote, "We must make our will conform in every respect to the will of God . . . So that we not only will what God wills, but also ought to will whatever God wills."[41] Lacan would reply that the obsessive already does this, and he cannot begin to imagine how much he misses by ignoring the already-present big Other. Recall the expanded matheme presented in the previous chapter ($S \diamond a \diamond A$), and imagine how much of Luther's theology (a) came from the big Other (A) he confused with more theology. In a roundabout way, Luther tried to resolve the judgment of the Law by returning the subject to the Law; we leave one version of the big Other for an(O)ther, but problem remains neurotically hazardous.

> Ecumenism only seems to have a chance if it is grounded in an appeal to the feebleminded.[42]

Excommunication provided the impetus for a more mature Luther. Pope Leo X issued the *Exsurge Domini* demanding recantation on June 15, 1520. The papal bull created a political crisis in the already-burgeoning factionalism of the Germanic countryside, for in the era before the modern nation state it was not clear whether the pope, the emperor, or the local Elector Frederick III (the Wise) had sovereignty over the territory's affiliation. The papal bull was all but inevitable after the Leipzig debate a year before, but ever since Luther continued to believe he could sway Rome's theological bulldog Johann Eck through debate. Eck rightly criticized Luther's plummeting view of papal authority, and Karl von Miltitz, long trusted as an intercessor in these matters, pleaded with Luther to settle the dispute before matters escalated to full excommunication. In a series of meetings, von Miltitz convinced Luther to agree to write a conciliator note to Leo X by mid-October. The open letter was politically savvy, and like all open letters, it was not meant for the gaze of its addressee. It was published in the vernacular German (which the pope could not himself read), and while it is entirely possible that one copy was sent to Rome, the letter proliferated

41. Luther, "Disputation against Scholastic Theology," 15.
42. Lacan, *Écrits*, 742.

quickly throughout the Germanic countryside. The letter was populist and posturing at its finest, meant to be read in the taverns and spread through Luther's affiliate publishers faster than a competing pamphlet by Eck.

The letter suggested the pope was victim, an honest man held captive by a wicked court. It alluded to a previous assassination attempt against Pope Leo, hinting to the watching public that even if his opinions were secretly with Luther, he could not say so for fear for his life. Luther claimed those who are faithful to Christ will necessarily curse the Curia, repeating the theme of caring more for the church than its hierarchs care. His Leipzig interlocutor entered the letter when "Satan opened his eyes and then filled his servant Johann Eck, a notable enemy of Christ, with an insatiable lust for glory and thus aroused him to drag me unawares to a debate, seizing me by means of one little word which I had let slip concerning the primacy of the Roman church."[43] Luther portrayed himself as Pope Leo's fellow victim of Eck and his cohort, and Luther proposed a conditional peace: "I detest contentions. I will challenge no one. On the other hand, I do not want others to challenge me. If they do, as Christ is my teacher, I will not be speechless."[44] The letter had a curious structure in proposing the impossible, made all the more impossible by it never really being proposed in the first place. It was pure posturing, first for the German countryside but ultimately for the eyes of one Elector Fredrick.

> For the man who breaks the bread of truth with his semblable in the act of speech shares a lie.[45]

If in fact the letter was ultimately for the eyes of Fredrick, the gamble appears to have worked. Luther burned the *Exsurge Domini* in a public display of defiance on December 10, 1520, and he was summarily excommunicated the following month. After the contentious Diet of Worms in May 1521 (concluding with the defiant, "Here I stand. I can do no other."), Fredrick's men intercepted Luther and relocated him safely to Wartburg. Luther began his translation of the New Testament into German and started a new phase of his career. It was not until excommunication was threatened that Luther could truly reorient his desires and understand that he and Rome were playing a different game. Language and mathemes are integrally transmitted from one person to the next, from ideologies to individuals, with or

43. Luther, "Freedom of a Christian," 338.
44. Ibid., 341.
45. Lacan, *Écrits*, 316.

without our knowledge.[46] Luther was obsessional neurotic in relationship with communal delusion of perverse fantasy. He was the fool for a collective knave until the relationship disintegrated. Luther almost certainly had no original intention of launching a Reformation, and like any sociopathic relationship it is possible Luther never would have cut ties had they not been cut for him. But in the end he had no choice, deprived of the master signifier of Roman eucharist. He was an outcast condemned to hell, and because of this he was free.

---

46. Lacan, *Encore*, 110.

Chapter 6

The Four Discourses
Universities, Masters, Hysterics, and Analysts

> Who can deny that philosophy has ever been anything other than
> a fascinating enterprise for the master's benefit?[1]

> I think this is the legacy of Christianity—this legacy of God not as
> a big Other or guarantee but God as the ultimate ethical agency
> who puts the burden on us to organize ourselves.[2]

LEO TOLSTOY ONCE OBSERVED that the complexity of an idea has no
bearing on whether it can be explained to the one willing to learn, but
for those persuaded they know already, no height of intelligence will surmount arrogance. Let us return to Adorno and Horkheimer's projection
theory of anti-Semitism: "Its horror lies in the fact that the lie is obvious
but persists. Though this deception allows no truth against which it could
be measured, the truth appears negatively in [the] very extent of the contradiction; and the undiscerning can be permanently kept from that truth
only if they are wholly deprived of the faculty of thought."[3] To deprive the
population of critical faculties is to produce a populism where everyone is
either friend or foe and nothing else.[4] Once we reach the point of populism,

---

1. Lacan, *Other Side of Psychoanalysis*, 23.
2. See Žižek, "A Meditation on Michelangelo's *Christ on the Cross*," 180.
3. Horkheimer and Adorno, *Dialectic of Enlightenment*, 208.
4. Ibid., 202.

whether in the political or theological realm, arguments cease to function as honest inquiry altogether.

We naïvely accept the dominance of ideologies through the master signifiers they produce. We are handed options from which to select, and after the selection is made we are forever in search of retroactive justifications. We need instead to think of ideologies in terms of (1) their production and (2) the truth revealed by what is produced, for as Karl Marx observed, "The philosophers have only *interpreted* the world in various ways; the point is, to *change* it."[5] The quote could be perceived as anti-intellectualism if one did not know its context. A more brutally straightforward version of this quote is often espoused as, "What is the point of endless philosophical debate?" Likewise, what is the point of theology? These questions, however reductionist and careless they may be, do confront us with a stark reality: for much of the time, there actually may be no point.

Whether or not there is a point to our work depends upon what the philosophy or theology is producing and the truth exposed in its production. In the second half of his seminar, having gained a popular Parisian following and consequent notoriety, Lacan altogether abandoned his early skepticism toward using psychoanalysis to think about social systems. *The Other Side of Psychoanalysis* brought his terminology firmly into the realm of the political and argued that we can analyze positions in society as one of four primary discourses: university, master, hysteric, and analyst. Each of these subdivide into four elements of agent, work, production, and truth. Economies subsequent social relations are a master's discourse, and we need to think of political theory and theology as a response to what occurs in these social relations. Whether the ideology plays the part of the master, the hysteric, the university, or the analyst depends chiefly on, again, (1) what it actually produces and (2) the truth exposed as the underside of that production.

> The more your quest is located on the side of truth, the more you uphold the power of the impossibles . . . governing, educating, analyzing on occasion.[6]

As much as ever, society operates as a mass of servants for the adoration of a select few masters. That this relationship is no longer legal but instead ingrained into the unconscious relations of economy makes the

5. Marx, "Theses on Feuerbach," 101.
6. Lacan, *Other Side of Psychoanalysis*, 187.

relationship all the more discrete. In *Debt*, David Graeber described the introduction of the debt economy as the tool by which those in power came to reframe their relationship to the underclasses as a moral issue. To reframe a financial arrangement as a moral imperative for the debtor relocates blame down the class ladder, and therefore the critical link between money and morality becomes the most important supporting tool for hegemonic interests to deploy. Power requires misrecognition, and misrecognition requires unconscious knowledge of what needs to be misrecognized.[7] Edelman describes politics as a name for "the space in which Imaginary relations, relations that hark back to a misrecognition of the self as enjoying some originary access to presence (a presence retroactively posited and therefore lost, one might say, from the start), compete for Symbolic fulfillment, for actualization in the realm of language to which subjectification subjects us all."[8] The emphasis is never on the direct misrecognition of the present so much as a misrecognition of a (mythic) past for which we can blame our present circumstances. "Politics, that is, names the struggle to effect a fantasmatic order of reality in which the subject's alimentation would vanish into the seamlessness of identity at the endpoint of the endless chain of signifiers lived as history."[9] This facet of the political domain is nothing new, but the requirement of misrecognition becomes all the more prominent under an mode of production that rewards nothing but excess: capitalism only functions as a death drive.

At its most basic level, an economy is a decision about how to divide limited resources. The critiques of capital relations exposed the conflicts under present conditions, but even alternative economic models retain problems within the subject. Everyone remains a captive of their egoist needs and their fundamental lack even if law successfully harmonized reason and need.[10] We accept inequality so long as we can frame it as some balance between effort and chance occurrence, but if psychoanalysis teaches us anything about repetition, it is that "there is nothing random in whatever we undertake with the intention of doing so at random."[11] Truth emerges from the mistake, and the mistake connects across a triad with the

---

7. Lacan, *Freud's Papers on Technique*, 167.

8. Edelman, *No Future*, 8.

9. Ibid.

10. Lacan, *Ethics of Psychoanalysis*, 208–9.

11. Lacan, *Ego in Freud's Theory*, 188.

lie and the position of ambiguity.[12] Analysis requires us to see in the error a trace of the truth.

> In fact, as the lie is organized, pushes out its tentacles, it requires the correlative control of the truth it encounters at every twist and turn of the way, and which it must avoid. The moralist tradition says it—you must have a good memory when you have lied.[13]

Consider Žižek's joke about a worker traveling for a job in Siberia. Before leaving, he promised to write to his friend of his new surroundings and proposed a way to evade the censorship of those surely reading the mail. He would write in blue ink if his description is true and red if false. After a while, the letter from Siberia arrived: "Everything is wonderful here: stores are full, food is abundant, apartments are large and properly heated, movie theaters show films from the West, there are many beautiful girls ready for an affair—the only thing unavailable is *red ink*."[14]

This suggests something about the insufficiency of language to critique the modes of thought producing that very language. Economy is but one example of how we lack the language to articulate our un-freedom, for we lack the conceptual tools to demolish the framework through which we are asked to decide the big questions. As Deleuze and Guattari wrote, "The fundamental problem of political philosophy is still precisely the one that Spinoza saw so clearly: 'Why do men fight *for* their servitude as stubbornly as though it were their salvation?'"[15] Spinoza wrote that a prophet produces a people, but have we today the tools to discern the prophet from the charlatan? The prophet is defiant; in the Hebraic tradition, one way to rule out a person as a legitimate prophet is to ask whether the more dogmatic religious authorities revile or celebrate the one who speaks.

> The atheist as a combatant and as a revolutionary is not one who denies God in his function of almightiness, he is one who affirms himself as not serving any god.[16]

12. Lacan, *Freud's Papers on Technique*, 228–29.

13. Ibid., 263.

14. Žižek, *Žižek's Jokes*, 95.

15. Deleuze and Guattari, *Anti-Oedipus*, 29, as quoted in Hardt and Negri, *Empire*, 210 (quote modified from the original).

16. Lacan, *Anxiety*, 309.

"Disobedience to authority," wrote Hardt and Negri, "is one of the most natural and healthy acts,"[17] and the question today is not why people rebel but instead why they do not. We should conceive of resistance as "communicating like a virus that modulates its form to find in each context an adequate host,"[18] but they observe the paradox of our supposedly most informed and connected digital age: the body is immunized against struggle, which is no longer communicable.

The state absorbs and domesticates the religion of its people, producing a latent political theology that undergirds the social strata and attaches itself to explicitly confessional theologies. The irony, as Hardt and Negri discuss, is that one could make a case for Christianity destroying the Roman Empire—eviscerating the civic passion mustered by the pantheon and criticizing loyalty to the Empire as nothing but idolatry—but Christianity too assimilated as a state religion before the fall came.[19] Ever since, power absorbs Christianity with ease, castrating its potential to become prophetic. Absorption into a master's discourse ensures theology has nothing to say. Power produces the need for a rigorous critique of theologies and politics, the efficaciousness of which Lacan always remained skeptical. There are masters, and there are slaves. But there are also the bureaucratic supports of the university opposed to the incisive critiques of analysts. We may select which of the latter two we desire to be, but we can only select one.

HEGEL'S MASTER AND SLAVE

> The morality of power, of the service of goods, is as follows: "As far as desires are concerned, come back later. Make them wait."[20]

The four discourses expand the master-slave dialectic Hegel developed in *Phenomenology of Spirit*. Hegel described consciousness as a *process*, a dialectic of interaction between the self and other selves, a process that recognizes the being-for-self of the other. Hegel used the lord-bondsman relationship to conceptualize consciousness at a time when the Haitian Revolution (the only slave revolt to ever end with a new state) weighed upon Europe. What were the colonizers to make of those asserting their

17. Hardt and Negri, *Empire*, 210.
18. Ibid., 51.
19. Ibid., 373.
20. Lacan, *Ethics of Psychoanalysis*, 315.

independent personhood? And could the next revolt be predicted? Politics since Athens had never found anything objectionable about slavery existing side-by-side with democracy, for the latter depended upon an underclass who could keep the work going while the elite called council. Bourgeois democracy required a deprived class. Quentin Lauer explained, "Hegel is not talking about an 'institution'; he is talking about what happens to the master-type of self-consciousness in the working out of this relationship."[21] Hegel was first of all talking about individuals, not history, though the historical implications are certainly there.

Truth is firstly a seduction, intended to deceive you.[22]

Consciousness desires the truth, or more to the point, we *think* we seek truth. But we can have certainty *or* truth; we cannot have both. Certainty-truth is always a process of becoming and never final, but arrogance seduces us into believing we have arrived. For Hegel the dialectical process of exposing truth never simply contradicts and does away with our old positions. The old positions are always lurking, and we embrace our embarrassing immaturity because it was instrumental in our process of learning. Hegel is often bastardized as promoting a moderate position that is nothing more that the lowest common denominator of synthesis between thesis and antithesis, but this neglects the need to genuinely retain the knowledge gained from brutally opposed positions. The dialectical process begins with (1) the negation of a position, (2) continues with the sublation of antagonisms into a new position, and (3) preserves the previous positions.

Understanding can only increase when the difference between two positions is made clear, when the antagonism is heightened. Anything other than a clear antagonism will descend into a battle over irrelevant semantics. We already implicitly understand this if we have ever debated ideas with someone holding a position we once held. The other person's view will tend to simply reduce our position to a different point of view on equal (though false) footing with her own perspective. But we will know our beliefs in a keenly different way than our friend could know, for where we are now is a product of once believing as the other believes currently. The process of production (whether of a product or an idea) changes our understanding of a matter in a way that conservation of the previous position cannot understand. For Hegel, this was a battle between the master's concern for

21. Lauer, *Reading of Hegel's Phenomenology of Spirit*, 130–31.
22. Lacan, *Other Side of Psychoanalysis*, 185.

what works and the slave's embedded and immanent knowledge of how something is working. Is the master concerned with how things work? Not at all. The master is only concerned that things go smoothly.[23]

> Work has never been given such credit ever since humanity has existed. It is even out of the question that one not work. This is surely an accomplishment of what I am calling the master's discourse.[24]

The one "in the know" is the one being churned by the machine. The slave is expendable. "This action of the [slave] is the [master's] own action; for what the bondsman does is really the action of the lord."[25] The master's identity depends on a slave in an asymmetrical way: the slave gains when freed, but the master depends on the slave for his status as master. Frustration builds, and the dialectic is trapped in stasis. Spinning the old proverb, Hegel agrees, "The fear of the fear of the lord is indeed the beginning of wisdom."[26] A life and death struggle for mutual recognition ensues where the slave has nothing to lose but life and the master, who has already lost his own soul, now stands to lose the world as well. "And it is only through staking one's life that freedom is won . . . The individual who has not risked his life may well be recognized as a *person*, but he has not attained to the truth of this recognition as an independent self-consciousness."[27] Hegel saw the threatening gesture as the point at which freedom can be incited, writing, "Without the discipline of service and obedience, fear remains at the formal stage, and does not extend to the known real world of existence."[28] But Lacan countered that the threatening gesture is often meant to be arrested and suspended.[29] There is a precise moment at which we can no longer handle abuse, but if the lord keeps the servant just shy of that incisive moment, repetition can continue indefinitely.

None of this struggle for recognition happens without brutality. The subjugation requires the fantasy of a big Other that produces an object *a* for the laborer to desire, and Lacan laments, Hegel's schema does nothing to

---

23. Ibid., 24.

24. Ibid., 168.

25. Hegel, *Phenomenology of Spirit*, 116.

26. Ibid., 117–18.

27. Ibid., 114.

28. Ibid., 119.

29. Lacan, *Four Fundamental Concepts of Psychoanalysis*, 116.

change the circumstances of slavery up until the eschatological moment.[30] So long as this fantasy remains in place uninterrupted, subjugation sustains itself without the need for force. The problem for the master is that the fantasy inevitably becomes interrupted. The subjugated learns through brutality that there is no hope for recognition from a master-system that depends on non-recognition, for the oppressor can only learn when he no longer has the option to ignore. This is why Žižek provocatively claims the worst slaveholders were the ones that were kind to their slaves. So long as subjugation exists, we hope to alleviate the suffering of the oppressed. This is a good thing. But we must always remember that wherever suffering is minimized, the need for change is correspondingly minimized. John Steinbeck perfectly captured the problem of antagonization minimization when he wrote that the problem for revolutionary politics is the absence of proletarians—everyone thinks herself a temporarily humiliated capitalist. Thus again, in society today we lack the very language to articulate our un-freedom.

THE PUPPET AND THE DWARF

To examine the four discourses, we should take an excursus into the political theology undergirding their use in this chapter. *The Other Side of Psychoanalysis* delves into the political realm, teasing his students radicalized by the protests of late-1960s Paris. Could the protest against the master produce anything other than a new master? Does the criticism of the big Other ever produce anything other than an(O)ther? Or worse than a new master, does the protester secretly wish to occupy the space of the new master? Joan Copjec explained, "To counter the romantic assumption that all institutions are necessarily confining and the voluntarist notion that the imagination would be free outside them, Lacan warns that the structures of institutions are not merely imposed on otherwise freely existing practices. All practices are always part of some institutional structure beyond which no practice, no critique, no speech is possible."[31] Though he remained somewhat skeptical, Copjec reminds her readers Lacan was influenced by the materialist position of N. Y. Marr, "who concluded that language was part of the superstructure, that is, that it was a direct reflection of class

30. Lacan, *Anxiety*, 23.

31. Lacan, *Television*, 51.

struggle, of the social determinations of the base."[32] Likewise, does our criticism of theology do anything more than produce a new bureaucratic support system for a voracious machine? Our expectations are rightly pessimistic, and as Heidegger lamented, only a God could save us.

We need to distinguish theological doctrine from its unconscious ideology. For Crockett, a radical political theology "means the attempt to sketch out a constructive theology that is neither liberal in a classic sense or conservative in any way, whether politically or theologically."[33] Theology and Law are at work in the unconscious in even the most secular society, though we delude ourselves into thinking we are free of ghosts by dismantling their conscious iterations. Ideology is the persistent and affective action that remains even if we were to subtract our rationale for that action. The concept of ideology is what allows us to say that regardless of your justifications and defenses for position x, you actually act as if you inhabit position y. Doctrine is not ideology in itself but instead the Imaginary expression of a latent, unconscious ideology. Crockett continues, "By linking theology with ideology, across a gap, I am also suggesting that a radical theology is necessarily a political theology. That is, radical theology necessarily finds itself informed and engaged with political conflicts and cannot simply appeal to a transcendent entity to escape or trump human social and political conversations and contestations."[34] The liberal illusion was that we could fully separate the religious from the political.

In his first thesis of *On the Concept of History*, Walter Benjamin wrote of a chess game in which every move was countered with a perfect move by an automaton. The automaton puppet puffed on its water pipe in the intervals between moves, creating the illusion of contemplation even though its calculated moves assured its eschatological victory. A system of mirrors created the illusion that one could see right through the table, but in fact a hunchbacked dwarf sat inside the puppet to control the game. One could imagine, Benjamin continued, that this is precisely our situation today, where the politics of historical materialism are merely a puppet controlled by a hidden theology. We suppose the material order will win the game, producing a revolutionary event or a messianic time, but what we get instead is a well-regulated technocracy supported by a theology, a term that means more after the twentieth century than the word's etymology suggests.

32. Ibid., 50.
33. Crockett, *Radical Political Theology*, 2.
34. Ibid., 41.

On the one hand, theology's confessional-religious forms (both in the strongman of the Religious Right and the weaker compassion of the Christian liberal) create a demographic that the politician must hear out even if it only desires to be co-opted. On the other hand, the specter of Schmitt's *Political Theology* tells us that modern political theory is nothing more than secularized theological concepts. We now call the nation state sovereign where we once called god sovereign, and where we once put faith in the priests we now put faith in currencies and uncritical presumptions concerning capital relations. The executive branch inherited the deity's power to force an exception to the rule. Schmitt joked (or perhaps we should be frightened that this is no joke), "today everything is theology, with the exception of what the theologians talk about."[35] Law creates lawbreakers *ex nihilo*; the moment of exception in the final moment of legal production cannot be justified by any means other than divine fiat.[36] Schmitt's observation is haunting, of course, because the faith of the patriot lead him to confidently ally himself with his own government in 1930s Germany.

In so many ways, Schmitt inscribed in political theory-as-theology what was already happening in the confessional theology of the German public. In several inter-war surveys, around 95 percent of the population identified as Christian. The standard reply among American Christians confronted with this fact today is that the Nazi Christian professed in bad faith. The excuse follows the pattern of a joke Lacan loved: my fiancée will never be late to meet me, because as soon as she is late she will no longer be my fiancée. The option to disavow the faith of another through a fetishized modification of doctrine clearly reduces the cognitive dissonance associated in sharing the faith of the Auschwitz guard, but more is going on than simple cognitive resistance. We should remember that *conscious resistance* is not the same as *unconscious censorship*. What is being censored in the unconscious in this hypothetical exchange is the terrible realization that Holocaust depended on Christian absolutism. It is only in the service of the Ultimate that we can justify the unforgivable. And thus in the face of the unforgivable, we try to reassert the Ultimate in vain. In his *The Puppet and the Dwarf*, Žižek reverses Benjamin's chess match to observe that in an age where radical thought is prohibited, we now play chess against explicitly theological matters that conceal the political agendas controlling its moves.

35. Taubes, *To Carl Schmitt*, 26.
36. Hardt and Negri, *Empire*, 16.

The Four Discourses

Imaginary ideologies directed by the big Other are proscribed from our awareness by illusions of secularity.

> In this new global order, religion has two possible roles: *therapeutic* or *critical*. It either helps individuals to function better in the existing order, or it tries to assert itself as a critical agency articulating what is wrong with this order as such, a space for the voices of discontent—in this second case, religion *as such* tends toward assuming the role of a heresy.[37]

We now move on to the four discourses—of the university, the master, the hysteric, and the analyst—and seek to turn the analysis back upon the monstrous chess game between the puppet and the dwarf. The mark that distinguishes the academic from the analyst is the ability to conceptualize questions outside of hegemonic boundaries, which we must do just as the psychoanalyst must do when wading through the analysand's infinitely altered stories that seek only to maintain the repetition of what does not work. And for a radical theology, Crockett writes, "Theology's estrangement is not estrangement from the world, the market, or contemporary society but primarily from *itself*. Radical theology risks such estrangement without the *assurance* that estrangement will be redeemed, whether provisionally or finally."[38] But if we take seriously the idea that theology is a second tier discourse, a method of speaking about something more fundamental, then the possibility that theological investigation kills itself off (or works itself out of a job) should be nothing to fear. We need to learn to ask better questions, and better questions always have a way of dismantling things. Learning to ask the proper question for the proper discourse might provide a guide, but I do not mean to give the reader a false hope—the outlook for theology is always grim.

37. Žižek, *Puppet and the Dwarf*, 3.
38. Crockett, *Interstices of the Sublime*, 100.

THE FOUR DISCOURSES

University	Master	Hysteric	Analyst
$S_2 \rightarrow a$	$S_1 \rightarrow S_2$	$\$ \rightarrow S_1$	$a \rightarrow \$$
$S_1 \quad \$$	$\$ \quad a$	$a \quad S_2$	$S_2 \quad S_1$

Positions		Terms	
Agent → Work		S_1: Master Signifier	S_2: Knowledge
Truth	Production	$\$$: Subject	a: object cause of desire

> Philosophy has played the role of constituting a master's knowledge, extracted from the slave's knowledge.[39]

In the beginning there were masters and slaves, and then came the support of universities and bureaucracies, and the analysts that had to choose a side. The schema begins at the top left's *agent* and reads clockwise around the four positions, proceeding to the space doing the actual *work* on the top right, and then resulting in the *product* on the bottom right. The remainder at the bottom left, the aftermath once the discourse churned out its production, is the revealing *truth* of the system. Signifiers have no natural hierarchy over another, but each takes the master signifier position by adopting the dominance of another's discourse.[40] Put differently, it matters not that we protest against the master if we are already shaped by the master's determinations.

> Culture, insofar as it is distinct from society, doesn't exist. Culture is the fact that it has a hold on us.[41]

Strictly speaking, the master signifier is empty and only has any value through the trust installed in it. It is established by fiat and seldom questioned afterward. Not unlike currencies, cultural ideals, or gods, the master signifier defines us not by being something measurable but by being the thing by which we measure everything else. The master is king because everyone wants to be a master (or at the least, everyone desires the *coup d'état* to install a new master), and the master needs our anger and envy to maintain power. So the master's discourse puts that envied status (S_1) to

39. Lacan, *Other Side of Psychoanalysis*, 148–49.

40. Ibid., 89.

41. Lacan, *Encore*, 53–54.

work (S_2). The laborer works for the master with the false hope that he too shall become an independent master over himself, and he and produces a desired product (a). The product is made to be consumed by the wage laborers in exchange for debts that return to the master. What is left over are the people ($\$$) churned up and robbed by the voracious economy, the people who wish they could be masters but will only ever by laborers.

> As soon as you raise the question, "What does So-and-so want?" you enter the function of desire, and you produce the master signifier.[42]

Notice that the truth position of each discourse is the agent position of the next. The master churns out new hysteric laborers. Laborers produce a need not only for therapists but (we hope) the desire for an analyst's discourse that could argue for a better social arrangement. The psychoanalyst's desire is what guides the analysand to understand their own unconscious desire, to separate what the subject desires from what she is told to desire. Analysts produce the insights needed for university discourse, but the intellectual elite too often produce nothing but a newly minted fuel for the master.

> Stupidity nevertheless has to be nourished.[43]

Christianity is in the interesting position of having a slavish and oppressed heritage that converted with Constantine to a master's discourse. Is this realization needed anywhere more than the United States today? The hegemonic superpower wherein capitalism and Christianity resonate such that no individual in the entire world is outside its reverberations—this is a true master's discourse. Yet because of perverse narratives aiming to keep its people subdued, American Christianity embraces an illusion of persecution. The fostered narrative's goal is always repetition, but repetition of what?

Lacan's surplus *jouissance* is Marx's surplus value. *Jouissance*, like capital, must be squandered.[44] Knowledge is the power to produce surplus (whether a surplus of value or surplus of *jouissance*), but production produces entropy.[45] A bit of knowledge escapes the master over time, and the

42. Lacan, *Other Side of Psychoanalysis*, 130.
43. Lacan, *Encore*, 14.
44. Lacan, *Other Side of Psychoanalysis*, 20.
45. Ibid., 50–51.

laborer—like the analysand beginning to see the patterns of repetition in her life—begins to learn something about the situation. The master today desires to keep the hysteric cheering, voting, and protesting in his favor. It is not enough for the neurotic public to be docile and subservient; active participation in one's own subjugation is demanded through clever schemes of tacit misinformation and outright propaganda deployed for the maintenance of a plutocracy. To distract from the system's aims, the very language needed to even begin to understand a political economy are denied to the crowds. Were we to survey popular understandings of capitalism, we would certainly see words such as liberty, democracy, the ability to by and sell and negotiate wages and start a business—all facets ironically describing many forms of socialism. What smallest fraction of our population could articulate proper definitions of economic, political, and religious systems that constitute their day to day interaction?

The master prefers his laborers never have the language to articulate any of this. William Connolly invokes the term "Evangelical-capitalist resonance machine" to describe resonances between money and religion, each with their disparate goals, which have produced a partnership to consolidate political and cultural power. A resonance certainly exists, but we are fools if we cannot see which one is the master in this relationship. In *Religion, Politics, and the Earth*, Clayton Crockett and Jeffrey W. Robbins engage this disinformation strategy in one of our chief masters today, and it is worth quoting at length:

> Should it be any surprise, after all, how easily aligned the Religious Right has become with a laissez-faire economic policy? . . . The neotraditionalist values-voter must surely recognize at least the tension, if not outright opposition, when their professed values run up against the relativization of all values that is the inevitable outcome of capitalism's making of money as the measure of all things . . . The same company that made stars of the likes of Bill O'Reilly and Sean Hannity run weekly parodies of their smallminded, loud-mouthed ways in the form of "Family Guy." In other words, it is not ideology that drives Fox News but crass capitalism. Whether selling smut or decrying it, the bottom line is the only value that maters. It is in this sense that we are speaking of the cynicism that passes for ethics today.[46]

---

46. Crockett and Robbins, *Religion, Politics, and the Earth*, 77.

HOSEA AND YAHWEH'S FEROCIOUS IGNORANCE

> People do History precisely in order to make us believe that it has
> some sort of meaning.[47]

In a perplexing lecture entitled "Yahweh's Ferocious Ignorance," Lacan asks whether a god is more like a master or an analyst. Scriptures always present a retrojected history to create a meaning for its people. Freud crafted peculiar counter-mythology of Moses the Egyptian (a successful utopian legislator killed by his people) and Moses the Midianite (a law-giver) and provoked his readers with the suggestion that guilt (over the murder of the leader) is what inscribed the law with such power. Indeed, the more we are guilty the more we censor our actions and thoughts, and we become more beholden to Law. There are any number of theories on the emergence of Yahweh and his relation to the Elohim of Canaanite mythology, but certainly the Tanakh would have us believe that Yahweh was the God of Abraham, Isaac, and Jacob.

In the story of Hosea, Yahweh decries Israel's infidelity with Baal by commanding Hosea to marry a prostitute whom he must continually reconcile with after her repeated affairs. Yahweh is a passionate and jealous God. Opposing Judaism to Buddhism, where passions are ideally purified from the individual, Lacan claims: "Love, hatred, and ignorance—there, in any case, are passions that are not absent from [Yahweh's] discourse."[48] Who in the ancient world could know whether or not sexual festivals convinced Baal to fertilize the earth? After all, the ritual did seem to work. We see a God who can be bartered with and convinced in stories of Abraham and Moses (a non-all-knowing God), but the ignorance in Hosea is a blind eye to patriarchy's reliance on the so-called oldest profession. In a world where prostitution was not only tacitly condoned but often important to religious rituals, and given the importance of temple worship to the emergence of ancient credit markets, we could easily imagine how contentious Yahweh appears in this story. It could be that Yahweh is ignorant of the sexual economy or ignorant of Baal's appreciation for the festivals. It could also be that Yahweh simply hates infidelity and cares for prostitutes. The Gaze is either blind toward the workings of the world, or instead the Gaze is ferociously full of rage. Either way, Hosea positions himself to be the neutral victim by

---

47. Lacan, *Encore*, 46.

48. Lacan, *Other Side of Psychoanalysis*, 136.

marrying a prostitute, demonstrating the unconscious desire of the community to commit adultery with so many gods.

The analyst is the one who is blind to supposed justifications on the one hand and ferociously opinionated on the other. The analyst must be neutral to the conscious justifications of the analysand but steadfast against the unconscious as it generates symptoms. Christian theology is at its best when it is an analyst's discourse, but outside of a select few strands of vociferously critical and shrewdly insightful conversations it has more often been a university discourse. The university discourse is the collective of knowledge that attracts us through an object of desire (a) which is some amalgamation of more knowledge and status. University discourse produces subjects (S) who too often become nothing more but cogs for the master's machine. The fourth position, the university's truth (S_1), is that it serves at the pleasure of the master.

To make matters far worse, religion typically dismisses its scholars and theorists and consigns them to their only paying possibility in academia. Christianity is rarely able to see its common position as a subservient neurotic, and populist folk religion safely separates itself from the university. In turn, folk religion produces its own folk theologies that no theologian could endorse while the broader Christian community believes these theologies to be normative, authoritative, and trustworthy. This creates a critical vacuum for the charlatan to fill. This confinement of scholarship and consequent emergence of folk theologies produces churches of fools beholden to theologies of knavery, and the theology of knavery is in turn the fool dependent upon the knavery of the political economy.

Let us return to Feuerbach's notion of religion as a projection and Žižek's claim that, though religion may be a false-consciousness, we should take it for granted that *all* consciousness is already a false-consciousness. If there is any insight whatsoever to the schema depicting subjectivity as a combination of big Other, subject, object a, and ego, we should take for granted the retrojected nature of everything from the simplest desire to the most complex ideology. Marx opined that religion exists a symptom of a problem rather than the problem itself, and who could reject this critique after the quickest cursory glance at higher rates of religious belief among the impoverished, among the oppressed, or among those who have no other recourse for hope in the moment of trauma? But I want to argue that Marxian religion-as-symptom isolates theology too squarely in the Imaginary register, something that can be identified and purged as a regressive instinct. Instead, if we at all desire to see theology do something useful after the materialist critique, we need to think (with Lacan, contra Marx) of theology as the expression of a death drive, which is always precariously balanced between self-destruction and creativity. Maintaining fidelity to Hegel, Lacan taught that while new perspectives generate from the analyst's discourse, the hope for change ultimately lies within the hysteric's discourse. The latter is prone to becoming co-opted, and we can only decide its efficacy in retrospect, for "there are historical events that can be judged only in terms of symptoms."[49]

Both in the instinctual mode of conservation and in the self-destructive mode of the death drive, theology maintains the status quo. It obsesses over absolutisms and speculative metaphysics and debates, and in its wake it leaves a wide swath of those marginalized and silenced. As I have said, my experience has been that people often find their own beliefs deplorable, untenable, even immoral, but they retain them because they feel they have to belief them; at the moment where we realize we do not have to believe anything in particular is the moment when theology alters course to the creative mode of the death drive. "What if, on the contrary," asks Crockett and Robbins, "religion had the capacity to subvert the status quo? In what ways has religion in fact functioned as a source of change?"[50] These two promote a new materialism that invites the chastening of the classic critiques while defying the idea that religion can (or even should) leave us. Theology is a language, but it is not always clear what that language means to get at. So perhaps the analyst should speak to the analysand in the language most accessible, which, it should go without saying, is not even remotely the same as deception. "In this way, the new materialist understanding of religion can be described as a form of 'sincere hypocrisy,' or of 'lying sincerely.'" I would comfortably claim Crockett and Robbins' "lying sincerely" or "sincere hypocrisy" as the creative mode of theology-as-drive, an insurrectionist theology for an "insurrectionist politics that takes the form of an occupation."[51] What we can be sure of is that lying happens regardless of its self-destructive or creative modes, and if progressive analysis of culture does not learn to speak the language of theology, "it will continue to cede territory and influence that should rightfully be its own."[52]

49. Lacan, *Television*, 124.

50. Crockett and Robbins, *Religion, Politics, and the Earth*, 25.

51. Ibid., 45.

52. Ibid., 31.

At this point in the early twenty-first century, the declining trend of American Christianity is clear to us, and its remainder (the discourse's "truth" position) is the "nones," those with no religious affiliation while at the same time often affirming so many elements of traditional theism. What the nones so often describe as reasons for leaving come down to folk theologies of their parents and grandparents, convinced as they are that Christian theology is too archaic to deal with matters of science or sexuality. And what is particularly frustrating for the theologian watching this is that these folk theologies are generally illegitimate to begin with. The average none's (former) pastor learned material in seminary that they ignore in the pulpit (perhaps for no other reason than careerism), and whether out of realism or idealism, the nones feel isolated by an antagonism that need not exist. Depth is lacking, and who could blame the one who walks away from experience without depth?

At the same time, American Evangelicalism is undergoing a resurgence of patriarchal, heterosexist, and fiercely dogmatic views. Perhaps resurgence is the wrong word if these views never really exited in the first place, but we can certainly see these views more out in the open in proud contrast to the broader liberal culture. The genus of modern Evangelicalism was the declining stature of fundamentalism in the 1930s, and the new Evangelicalism sought to maintain what it saw as fundamentalist beliefs without the air of hostility characterizing its forerunner. That is changing with the resurgence of dogmatism. That this should happen now—in a time of globalization, significant cultural restructuring, economic insecurity and corresponding conditions of our new permanent state of war—is not surprising. And neither is it all that surprising to see the Evangelical-capitalist resonance machine of late-capitalism reach new heights of co-option. What I do find interesting is that resurgent fundamentalism arose concurrent with unprecedented access to information. All knowledge is accessible through a smartphone in seconds after a question rises, but we lack either the ability to organize that information or the desire to see. Algorithms are our new big Other, tailoring results to our biases. When the voter or parishioner suspects she is hearing less than the full truth from the leader, she has only to conduct a cursory internet search to confirm her suspicion. But rather than a great awakening of religious, economic, political, and cultural knowledge, we opted instead to entrench ourselves like never before into tribalism.

I previously introduced this pattern: *perversion pressures neurosis to reorient specifically as obsessionalism, often through hysteric or psychotic language.* The knave understands its community to lack something and imagines itself to provide the object *a.* Thus for the fundamentalist leader, the imagined patriarchal solution for feminized culture requires him to over-project the masculinity he believes to be the missing object. This is merely an internal conflict projected outward. But the parishioners, if they occupy the position of the fool, will see certainty not as the reflection of an internal conflict or prejudice but instead as the reflection of the will of a god. Observing contemporary Evangelical language, one often wonders whether the believer really imagines their metaphors could mean anything at all concrete. The language displays hysterical or psychotic traits, but it is not because Christianity is necessarily hysterical or psychotic (although to express its best potential, religion *should* be hysterical, for this is the lesson of Hegel and Lacan). The language is exchangeable; the moment we hear religious language that cannot convert to saying anything concrete, we are more likely hearing what the knave desires to hear rather than what the normally-adjusted neurotic parishioner would independently generate.

The knave's ideal fool is the obsessional who depends on the Other to tell her what to desire; if the perverse Other can ideologically subjugate the obsessive by demanding insider language more consistent with hysteria or psychosis, so be it. The language is irrelevant; the master only cares that things work smoothly. It is left to those of us who do this work to put our own interests at risk by exposing the antagonisms and to deny the pressure to buy in to the deplorable. But we can only do this from the unsafe position of the analyst.

ANALYSTS AND BUREAUCRATS: KNOWLEDGE, TRUTH, AND OPINION

> In other words, the only criticism I have to make of you, if I may,
> is that you all want to appear too clever.[53]

Interpretation is always established through enigma.[54] At some point, the analyst must speak, and when she does so she commits herself with the full knowledge that she may speak too soon and thus render her work

53. Lacan, *Ego in Freud's Theory*, 27.
54. Lacan, *Other Side of Psychoanalysis*, 37.

ineffective beyond repair. The analysand may leave the session, she may incorporate the interpretation into her repetition, or she may descend into hopelessness. We do the same with the interpretation of the text, praying our interpretation bears fruit even among the endless contingencies that guarantee our interpretation is never definitely or finally correct. Interpretations will always require revision, and no amount of revision can altogether avoid unforeseen harm. Interpretation always establishes a point of enigmatic rejection. Indeed, all of Lacan's ethics could be summed up as such: the ethical absolutely cannot be *this*, the big Other's demand—there must be a better way.

> To be truthful, it is only from where knowledge is false that it is concerned with the truth. All knowledge that is not false couldn't give a damn about it.[55]

Knowledge is easy enough to access and deploy. Knowledge is merely signifiers coming together through an enigma to establish a metonymic idea, a conception of how things surely must operate. Knowledge is raw data; truth is how that data is used for the subject. And the truth for many subjects and systems is that they are nothing but knaves, or worse, that they are expendable fools working for a knave. The opposition is not between knowledge and truth. The opposition is between (1) the truth of how the subject actually operates and (2) how the subject forms opinions to justify how she operates. Truth is always unconscious in the Real; opinion is retrojected illusion. The analyst will always have a pernicious tendency to correct opinions as if the opinion itself is the disease. The opinion is not the disease. The regressive belief is not the disease. The analyst must learn to treat the unconscious source, which is only expressed indirectly through the symptom of speech. Knowledge is the Symbolic gap between the truth and opinion, and it is in that knowledge gap that the analyst must position herself.

> What is troublesome is that when it comes to the monkey ladder, as you put your feet on one rung, you forget the steps below—or you let them rot.[56]

The pernicious tendency of the academy is to pull up the ladder behind us, the ladder that we climbed up and benefited from yet now deny to others. The university discourse isolates itself from common parlance,

55. Ibid., 186.
56. Lacan, *Ego in Freud's Theory*, 28.

and in so doing, Lacan laments, the human sciences outlive their usefulness by forging their servitude to the master's technocracy.[57] We lament that so many centuries of philosophical posturing and religious hypocrisy have contributed so little to understanding "the man of humanism and the irremediably contested debt he has incurred against his intentions."[58] In the field of theology this has created a near infinite space for folk theologies that serious theologians—now irrelevant and impotent due to self-selected isolation—must continuously skirmish against with the precision tool of knowledge that rarely surmounts the mass-destruction weapons of content-free opinion. Knowledge collapses into foolish production, and the Real remains untouched. The trauma of what does not work will dust itself off and wait for the next crisis, *ad infinitum*.[59] What is to be done?

The analyst's discourse can only surmount the public's attraction to content-free opinion by recovering its potential as something desired (a) by the proletarian masses. The analyst must put her capabilities to work with conversations and writings for the masses (S) that eviscerate the co-opted purposes of religion (personal meaning and tribal cohesion), and the analyst can only do this when she risks loosing her status as anything desirable (a). Indeed, any critique worth listening to will always seem intrusive and hostile in the beginning, for if we do not seem hostile at times, then perhaps we have nothing to say. But if there is any success in what we have to say to the mass of subjects (S), we produce new kinds of master signifiers (S_1), and the truth (S_2) of our work will be that we have created knowledge worth hearing. If theology does not produce new master signifiers for thinking about our relations, it has only handed officially sanctioned and foolish identities over to the knave's mechanistic identity politics.

God only knows, the knave does not give a damn about our theologies so long as they produce new fools. If producing new fools for use by old knaves is our only outcome, we ought to give up sooner rather than later. Throughout this chapter, I referenced Lacan's pessimism regarding the ability for radicalism and university discourse to produce the analysis we so terribly need. We might make progress, but our tendency is to emulate the past. Though a leftist himself, he famously concluded there was little hope for radicals:

57. Lacan, *Écrits*, 730.
58. Ibid., 349.
59. Lacan, *Other Side of Psychoanalysis*, 186.

If you had a bit of patience, and if you really wanted our impromptus to continue, I would tell you that, always, the revolutionary aspiration has only a single possible outcome—of ending up as the master's discourse. This is what experience has proved. What you aspire to as revolutionaries is a master. You will get one.[60]

60. Ibid., 207.

Chapter 7

The Prophet and the Charlatan

If there is one thing that psychoanalysis should force us to maintain obstinately, it's that the desire for knowledge bears no relation to knowledge.[1]

We must be ready, too, to abandon a path that we have followed for a time, if it seems to be leading to no good end. Only believers, who demand that science shall be a substitute for the catechism they have given up, will blame an investigator for developing or even transforming his views.[2]

I HAVE ALWAYS LOVED a quote from Nietzsche on the criticism of dark gods: "I love him who chastens his god because he loves his god: for he must perish of the wrath of his god."[3] It is remarkable that materialist critiques of religion have produced such cogently perceptive theology over the last two centuries. Perhaps this should be expected if Schmitt was correct that, today, everything is theological except what the theologians proclaim to be such. It seems that Marx foresaw the rise of analysis and political theology when he wrote, "Thus the *criticism of heaven* turns into the *criticism of the earth*, the *criticism of religion* into the *criticism of law*, and the *criticism of theology* into the *criticism of politics*."[4] The gods do not

1. Ibid., 23.
2. Freud, "Beyond the Pleasure Principle," 626.
3. Nietzsche, "Thus Spoke Zarathustra," 128.
4. Marx, "Toward a Critique of Hegel's *Philosophy of Right*: Introduction," 28–29.

really die, but they shift forms. We evolved with a need to believe, and if a god appears to die an(O)ther will occupy the vacated position. We are forever rearranging and re-articulating the Imaginary to account for flaws in the Symbolic; we do not even touch the Real (to say nothing of reality as such). This book has shied from a constructive theology. Just as the ethics of psychoanalysis have little to say about what is ethical but much of what the ethical cannot be, a psychoanalytic protest theology can only say there must be a better way to think.

Lacan took it for granted that Christianity would triumph over psychoanalysis. He displayed remarkable certainty when compared with the Žižek, who does not at all take Christianity's continued existence for granted. Through his reading of Saint Paul, Žižek unapologetically argues we have reached a critical moment where social progress and radical politics need Christian theology more than ever. It is an ecclesiology of sorts wherein the emancipatory path to repairing the world can only come through the communities that operate in a state of godforsakenness. We must operate without the contrived security of a big Other providing teleo-logical guarantees of success: "I claim that if we lose this key moment—the moment of realizing the Holy Spirit as a community of believers—we will live in a very sad society, where the only choice will be between vulgar egoist liberalism or the fundamentalism that counterattacks it."[5] It is difficult to know precisely what early Christian communities felt themselves to orga-nize around, for the gospel of Saint Paul clearly had its differences from the gospel of Christ; what we see without equivocation is a community bound by an ideal. Radically emancipatory thought should not cede ground that is rightfully its own. Christianity, Žižek claims, "is far too precious a thing to leave to conservative fundamentalists. We should fight for it. Our message should not be, 'You can have it,' but 'No, it's ours. You are kidnapping it.'"[6]

Unfortunately, it is all too easy to kidnap an opaque idea when truth always has the structure of a fiction. Opacity bears the possibility of creat-ing meaning *ex nihilo*, but the position is always precariously open. Perhaps it is the case that Žižek and I alike create a meaning from Lacan that he himself would reject in the same way that liberalism and fundamentalism fashion a version of Christ that did not exist. The fundamentalist fails to recognize the rather obvious reality that Christ was always opposed to the dogmatic religious types of his day. The liberal fails to recognize that,

5. See Žižek, "Meditation on Michelangelo's *Christ on the Cross*," 181.
6. Ibid., 181.

however emancipatory Christ was in his moment, the idea of God should continuously be far more radicalized than the liberal dream of slight legal shifts within a basically stable social or economic regime. When someone worth listening to speaks, the word will be cryptic enough to be meaningful, which is to say it will be cryptic enough to be misinterpreted. There is no teleological guarantee.

WHY DOES A PLANET NOT SPEAK?

Lacan first introduced the big Other as a commentary on *Mein Kampf*. Hitler wrote of men as moons in orbit around a body, disturbing each other with a mutual gravitational pull. It is such a bizarre question with which he introduces the big Other: why does a planet not speak?[7] Analysts, scientists, and politicians all face the temptation to reduce their subjects to moons whose movements, masses, and gravitation can be calculated and predicted. Calculation of this kind requires a certain baseline emotional state, but when again is it that we are our normal selves? If we are happy, is that more or less us than when we are depressed? And what are we to make of our happiness that results only from the happiness of another? "This relation of the subject's satisfaction with the satisfaction of the other—to be understood, please, in its most radical form—is always at issue where man is concerned . . . There is no image of identity, of reflexivity, but a relation of fundamental alterity."[8] We are always in orbit. But why do planets in orbit not speak? First, a planet has nothing to say. Second, it not the time to say anything. Third, it has been silenced.

If we receive the answer we were expecting, is it really an answer?[9]

We are silenced because we, like the planet, do not have a mouth. We begin our careers without credibility or respect, fighting the impostor syndrome while knowingly faking our confident expertise. The stars are always out there in their place—the Real and the gods are always in their place—but an orbit is constantly in reciprocal influence. Lacan brought Heisenberg's principle into analysis to say we can only speak of an idea if we no longer know where that idea is going to take us: "I am not saying that we will always be in this eminently ludicrous position. But until things

7. Lacan, *Ego in Freud's Theory*, 235.
8. Ibid., 236.
9. Ibid., 237.

change, we can say that the elements don't answer where one asks them. More precisely, if one asks them somewhere, it is impossible to grasp them as a whole."[10] To analyze the residues of authentic action is to see something new emerge.[11]

We mapped the stars with Orion, the Pleiades, and the Great Bear to find our way, and it mattered not that the symbolism was entirely fictional. Copernicus and Newton put the mystery of movement to death and gave calculation to what had evaded understanding for all of human history to up to that moment. Einstein taught us that while the Almighty was crafty, the Almighty was not dishonest. But to keep its honesty, to truly remove the element of surprise from the universe, the Almighty was shut up in silence. The Other was shut up, not just because planets and stars were dumb masses but because inscription into a language of a unified field and gravitation reduced the heavens to three small letters: Law.

We would be moons if we could simply reduce ourselves to laws and doctrines. What makes us human is our constitutive false consciousnesses. We have the ability to lie and to deceive ourselves, which is the only reason truly intersubjective relationships can exist.[12] A false reality can still be a verified reality. The Imaginary register produces an ego (a) that will interact other egos (a_1, a_2, a_3, etc.) through language founded upon big Others (A_1, A_2, A_3, etc.). We see ourselves the way we see others, that is to say, we are unsure of who we are or what motivates our desires. The analyst should be an empty mirror for the analysand. "The analysis consists in getting him to become conscious of his relations, not with the ego of the analyst, but with all these Others who are his true interlocutors, whom he hasn't recognized."[13] What is resisted by the conscious is repeated in the act.[14] The unconscious *insists* on repetition. The big Other is nonexistent, but it insists with a clamoring, voracious appetite, a *je-ne-sais-quoi*-drive.[15] Saint Augustine asked what he loved when he loved his God, for this is always the question one poses to the big Other: who are you, and what do you want?

> The symbolic order is simultaneously non-being and insisting to
> be, that is what Freud has in mind when he talks about the death

10. Ibid., 240.
11. Ibid.
12. Ibid., 244.
13. Ibid., 246.
14. Lacan, *Four Fundamental Concepts of Psychoanalysis*, 51.
15. Lacan, *Ego in Freud's Theory*, 325.

[drive] as being what is most fundamental—a symbolic order in travail, in the process of coming, insisting on being realized.[16]

FATHER, CAN'T YOU SEE THAT I AM BURNING?

There is a famously horrific episode Freud wrote of as confirmation of his thesis in *The Interpretation of Dreams*. A young boy died and his body was placed in an adjacent room as the father rested after the traumatic day. While asleep, a candle was knocked over and set the boy's room ablaze. The trauma of loss and the scent of smoke entwined in the father's dream-state, and he saw his son approach his bed and lean over to quietly whisper, *Father, can't you see that I am burning?* The father immediately awoke in sheer panic, but why? He awoke precisely to stay asleep, and our waking activity is often nothing but the avoidance of what lurks in the unconscious.

> Desire manifests itself in the dream by the loss expressed in an image at the most cruel point of the object. It is only in the dream that this truly unique encounter can occur. Only a rite, an endlessly repeated act, can commemorate this not very memorable encounter—for no one can say what the death of a child is, except the father qua father, that is to say, no conscious being.[17]

We are faced again with something analogous to the prefiguration of Christ in Job's demand that that Symbolic provide an answer that cannot be provided. Žižek observed, "Is Christ's 'Father, why have you forsaken me?' not the Christian version of Freud's 'Father, can't you see I am burning?'? And is this not addressed precisely to God-Father who pulls the strings behind the stage and teleologically justifies (guarantees the meaning of) all our earthly vicissitudes? Taking upon himself (not the sins, but) the suffering of humanity, he confronts the Father with the meaninglessness of it all."[18] The big Other only learns by being made to suffer, for maturity is a process of learning every big Other is a false god.

What is a dream? What is a religious rite? A dream is not simply a fantasy fulfilled by a particular wish.[19] A dream is an organization around a

---

16. Ibid., 326.

17. Lacan, *Four Fundamental Concepts of Psychoanalysis*, 59.

18. See Žižek, "Fear of Four Words: A Modest Plea for the Hegelian Reading of Christianity," 57.

19. Lacan, *Four Fundamental Concepts of Psychoanalysis*, 59.

reality that is missing, a reality that can only exist in repetition. Lacan wrote of religion, art, and science as, respectively, obsessional neurosis, hysteria, and psychosis. Science must always at once (1) depend on the Symbolic formulas that direct its research and (2) conflate the formula with the Real. A paradigm shift occurs when the Symbolic can no longer account for the weighty intrusions of the Real. So just as psychosis *forecloses* on the Symbolic, the sciences must always maintain an element of denial that postpones a confrontation with the void of the Real for as long as possible.

> The rationalism organizing theological thought is in no way a matter of fancy, as the platitude would have it. If there is fantasy therein, it is in the most rigorous sense of the institution of a real that covers (over) the truth.[20]

On the other hand, religion and art organize themselves in relationship to the void. Recall that obsessionalism is submission to the big Other's injunction whereas hysteria sabotages it, which results in direct desire as impossible for the obsessive and unsatisfied for the hysteric.[21] Is the hysteric's overload of information-transfer to the analyst so very different from the paint covering a canvass, an organization around an emptiness?[22] Art is at its best when it flirts with interpretations and evades a definite stance. A caption defining the correct interpretation dissolves its ability to speak and reduces it to propaganda. Art must embrace its hysteria.

But religion is something altogether different. The big Other can only be spoken of as a question of faith or feint.[23] Theology explicitly organizes itself at the edge of the void, speaking precariously (and hopefully cautiously) about the ineffable. Art is a derivative of repression, and religion is a sublimation or displaced derivative of repression.[24] Religion speaks at reality not directly but from the flank. Just as the obsessive may go to analysis already knowing the correct course of action while hoping this course will not be named by the analyst, religion prays its fictions will not be exposed. So long as its theological network of identity-stabilizing signifiers remains intact, even the worst of dehumanizing beliefs can reduce the believer's anxiety. The religious rite—like a dream or like the representative in the place of

20. Lacan, *Écrits*, 741.

21. Ibid., 571.

22. Lacan, *Ethics of Psychoanalysis*, 136.

23. Lacan, *Psychoses*, 69.

24. Lacan, *Ethics of Psychoanalysis*, 131.

a representation—is an organization around what cannot be named, a covering-over of anxiety, a representative in the place of a representation. The object *a* is no-being, "a void presupposed by a demand."[25] Religion says God is ineffable, but this is not quite so. We can speak of gods all day long; what must remain ineffable is the void the gods cover.

> For the true formula of atheism is not God is dead . . . the true formula of atheism is God is unconscious.[26]

CONSUME THE BOOK

In the tenth chapter of Revelation, an angel descended from the heavens with a countenance like the sun and feet like pillars of fire. The angel stood with one foot on the seas and the other on the earth. The angel roared like a lion and the skies thundered, but a voice from the heavens commanded that the message never be written. After the silencing, the angel cried out that cosmic time was finished, that the mystery of God should soon be revealed to the prophets who have ears to hear. The voice from the heavens commanded the man to take a book from the angel's hand and eat it. The book tasted sweet as honey but was bitter to the stomach. Likewise, the message that must be prophesied to kings and nations will appear sweet but end in bitterness.

> When in the Apocalypse we read this powerful image, "eat the book," what does it mean?—if it isn't that the book itself acquires the value of an incorporation, the incorporation of the signifier itself, the support of the properly apocalyptic creation. The signifier in this instance becomes God, the object of the incorporation itself.[27]

This book began with a story of Freud and Jung gazing upon the statue as they sailed to their reception in New York. Was it hubris or prescience to suggest their ideas would so disrupt what we thought we understood about ourselves? Our experience is often one of wishing we could go back and un-learn the things we found ourselves more at peace without knowing.

25. Lacan, *Encore*, 126.
26. Lacan, *Four Fundamental Concepts of Psychoanalysis*, 59.
27. Lacan, *Ethics of Psychoanalysis*, 294.

The haunting words shadow us: "They don't realize we're bringing them the plague."[28]

Nietzsche asked what was left to be said after the death of God?—we the murderers of all murderers, who will wash holy blood of our hands? How now does the *Übermensch* cope with anxiety when there can be no festivals of atonement? This is our question today, for where does society turn when it can no longer name the big Other? The answer, of course, is that gods do not die but instead only change forms; if gods could die, they would know it. Belief gets into us, and it stays with us irrevocably.

In *The Triumph of Religion*, Lacan entertained a series of questions from a poor journalist. Was he a philosopher? "I am not a philosopher, not in the least."[29] What was your distinct message? "I have never claimed to have discovered anything."[30] Why write so incomprehensibly? "People don't understand anything, that is perfectly true, for a while, but the writings do something to them."[31] And what if nobody had ears to hear? "I'm not afraid of people leaving. On the contrary, I am relieved when they leave."[32] Will psychoanalysis become a religion? "Psychoanalysis? No. At least I hope not . . . psychoanalysis is a symptom."[33] Over and over, the analyst evades the expected answer, refusing to settle a question on the terms it proposes. But the question of a battle being waged between psychoanalysis and religion elicits no such evasion.

> [Religion] will triumph not only over psychoanalysis but over lots of other things too. We can't even begin to imagine how powerful religion is . . . Religion, above all the true religion, is resourceful in ways we cannot even begin to suspect.[34]

Lacan is sometimes treated as a prophet and sometimes dismissed as a charlatan. To say anything worth saying usually guarantees the application of both labels. And theory is always like this, oscillating between the incisively perceptive and the merely ludicrous—the analyst should rightly think herself mad at times. In the end we are thrown into a world we mark

28. Lacan, *Écrits*, 336.
29. Lacan, *Triumph of Religion*, 80.
30. Ibid., 75.
31. Ibid., 70.
32. Ibid., 85.
33. Ibid., 65.
34. Ibid., 64.

with signifiers, and those signifiers mark us right back. When we face the command to consume a book, we will surely fall ill with a bitter plague.

> "Is he good, is he bad?" That question now seems unimportant. The important thing is not knowing whether man is good or bad in the beginning; the important thing is what will transpire once the book has been eaten.[35]

35. Lacan, *Ethics of Psychoanalysis*, 325.

Bibliography

Brewin, Kester. *Mutiny! Why We Love Pirates, and How They Can Save Us*. London: Vaux, 2012.

Caputo, John D. *The Insistence of God: A Theology of Perhaps*. Bloomington: Indiana University Press, 2013.

Crockett, Clayton. *Interstices of the Sublime: Theology and Psychoanalytic Theory*. New York: Fordham University Press, 2007.

———. *Radical Political Theology: Religion and Politics after Liberalism*. New York: Columbia University Press, 2011.

Crockett, Clayton, and Jeffrey W. Robbins. *Religion, Politics, and the Earth: The New Materialism*. New York: Palgrave Macmillan, 2012.

Dobbin, Robert, ed. *The Cynic Philosophers from Diogenes to Julian*. New York: Penguin Classics, 2012.

Edelman, Lee. *No Future: Queer Theory and the Death Drive*. Durham, NC: Duke University Press, 2004.

Feuerbach, Ludwig. *The Essence of Religion*. Translated by Alexander Loos. Amherst, NY: Prometheus, 2004.

Fink, Bruce. *A Clinical Introduction to Lacanian Psychoanalysis: Theory and Technique*. Cambridge: Harvard University Press, 1997.

Foucault, Michel. *Discipline and Punish: The Birth of the Prison*. Translated by Alan Sheridan. New York: Vintage, 1977.

Freud, Sigmund. "Beyond the Pleasure Principle." In *The Freud Reader*, edited by Peter Gay, 594–626. New York: Norton, 1989.

———. *Civilization and Its Discontents*. Translated by Joan Riviere. Mansfield Centre, CT: Martino, 2010.

———. "The Ego and the Id." In *The Freud Reader*, edited by Peter Gay, 631–58. New York: Norton, 1989.

———. *The Future of an Illusion*. Translated by W. D. Robson-Scott. Mansfield Centre, CT: Martino, 2011.

———. "Instincts and Their Vicissitudes." In *The Freud Reader*, edited by Peter Gay, 562–68. New York: Norton, 1989.

———. *Jokes and Their Relation to the Unconscious*. Translated by James Strachey. New York: Norton, 1960.

———. "Obsessive Actions and Religious Practices." In *The Freud Reader*, edited by Peter Gay, 429–36. New York: Norton, 1989.

Bibliography

————. "Repression." In *The Freud Reader*, edited by Peter Gay, 568–72. New York: Norton, 1989.

Hardt, Michael, and Antonio Negri. *Empire*. Cambridge: Harvard University Press, 2001.

Hegel, G. W. F. *Phenomenology of Spirit*. Translated by A. A. Miller. New York: Oxford University Press, 1977.

Heschel, Abraham Joshua. *God In Search of Man: A Philosophy of Judaism*. New York: Farrar, Straus and Giroux, 1955.

Horkheimer, Max, and Theodor W. Adorno. *Dialectic of Enlightenment*. Translated by John Cumming. New York: Herder and Herder, 1972.

King, Barbara J. *Evolving God: A Provocative View of the Origins of Religion*. New York: Doubleday, 2007.

Krips, Henry. *Fetish: An Erotics of Culture*. Ithaca: Cornell University Press, 1999.

Kuhn, Thomas S. *The Structure of Scientific Revolutions*. 3rd ed. Chicago: University of Chicago Press, 1996.

Lacan, Jacques. *Anxiety: The Seminar of Jacques Lacan, Book X*. Edited by Jacques-Alain Miller. Translated by A. R. Price. Malden, MA: Polity, 2014.

————. *Écrits: The First Complete Edition in English*. Translated by Bruce Fink. New York: Norton, 1996.

————. *The Ego in Freud's Theory and in the Technique of Psychoanalysis, 1954–1955: The Seminar of Jacques Lacan, Book II*. Edited by Jacques-Alain Miller. Translated by Sylvana Tomaselli. New York: Norton, 1991.

————. *Encore, 1972–1973, On Feminine Sexuality, the Limits of Love and Knowledge: The Seminar of Jacques Lacan, Book XX*. Edited by Jacques-Alain Miller. Translated by Bruce Fink. New York: Norton, 1998.

————. *The Ethics of Psychoanalysis 1959–1960: The Seminar of Jacques Lacan, Book VII*. Edited by Jacques-Alain Miller. Translated by Dennis Porter. New York: Norton, 1997.

————. *The Four Fundamental Concepts of Psychoanalysis: The Seminar of Jacques Lacan, Book XI*. Edited by Jacques-Alain Miller. Translated by Alan Sheridan. New York: Norton, 1981.

————. *Freud's Papers on Technique, 1953–1954: The Seminar of Jacques Lacan, Book I*. Edited by Jacques-Alain Miller. Translated by John Forrester. New York: Norton, 1991.

————. *My Teaching*. Translated by David Macey. New York: Verso, 2008.

————. *On the Names-of-the-Father*. Translated by Bruce Fink. Malden, MA: Polity, 2013.

————. *The Other Side of Psychoanalysis: The Seminar of Jacques Lacan, Book XVII*. Edited by Jacques-Alain Miller. Translated by Russell Grigg. New York: Norton, 2007.

————. *The Psychoses, 1955–1956: The Seminar of Jacques Lacan, Book III*. Edited by Jacques-Alain Miller. Translated by Russell Grigg. New York: Norton, 1993.

————. *Television: A Challenge to the Psychoanalytic Establishment*. Edited by Joan Copjec. New York: Norton, 1990.

————. *The Triumph of Religion*. Translated by Bruce Fink. Malden, MA: Polity, 2013.

Laertius, Diogenes. *Lives of the Philosophers*. Edited by A. Robert Caponigri. Chicago: Regnery, 1969.

Lauer, Quentin. *A Reading of Hegel's Phenomenology of Spirit*. New York: Fordham University Press, 1976.

Bibliography

Luther, Martin. "Disputation against Scholastic Theology." In *Career of the Reformer: I*, edited and translated by Harold J. Grimm, 3–16. Luther's Works 31. Philadelphia: Muhlenberg, 1957.

———. "The Freedom of a Christian." In *Career of the Reformer: I*, edited by Harold J. Grimm, translated by A. W. Lambert, 327–77. Luther's Works 31. Philadephia: Fortress, 1957.

———. "The Large Catechism." In *The Book of Concord: Confessions of the Evangelical Lutheran Church*, edited by Robert Kolb and Timothy J. Wengert, translated by Charles Arand et al., 377–480. Minneapolis: Fortress, 2000.

Marx, Karl. "Theses on Feuerbach." In *Karl Marx: Selected Writings*, edited by Lawrence H. Simon, 99–101. Indianapolis: Hackett, 1994.

———. "Toward a Critique of Hegel's *Philosophy of Right*: Introduction." In *Karl Marx: Selected Writings*, edited by Lawrence H. Simon, 28–39. Indianapolis: Hackett, 1994.

Nietzsche, Friedrich. "Thus Spoke Zarathustra." In *The Portable Nietzsche*, edited and translated by Walter Kaufman, 121–439. New York: Penguin, 1976.

Pew Research Center for the People and the Press. "Public Sees a Future Full of Promise and Peril." http://www.people-press.org/2010/06/22/public-sees-a-future-full-of-promise-and-peril.

Sandeen, Ernest R. *The Roots of Fundamentalism: British and American Millenarianism 1800–1930*. Chicago: University of Chicago Press, 1970.

Taubes, Jacob. *To Carl Schmitt: Letters and Reflections*. Translated by Keith Tribe. New York: Columbia University Press, 2013.

Žižek, Slavoj. *Did Somebody Say Totalitarianism? Five Interventions in the (Mis)use of a Notion*. New York: Verso, 2001.

———. "The Fear of Four Words: A Modest Plea for the Hegelian Reading of Christianity." In *The Monstrosity of Christ: Paradox or Dialectic?*, edited by Creston Davis, 24–109. Cambridge: MIT Press, 2009.

———. *How to Read Lacan*. New York: Norton, 2006.

———. "A Meditation on Michelangelo's *Christ on the Cross*." In *Paul's New Moment: Continental Philosophy and the Future of Christian Theology*, edited by Creston Davis, 169–81. Grand Rapids: Brazos, 2010.

———. *The Parallax View*. Cambridge: MIT Press, 2006.

———. "Paul and the Truth Event." In *Paul's New Moment: Continental Philosophy and the Future of Christian Theology*, edited by Creston Davis, 74–99. Grand Rapids: Brazos, 2010.

———. *The Puppet and the Dwarf: The Perverse Core of Christianity*. Cambridge: MIT Press, 2003.

———. *Žižek's Jokes: Did You Hear the One about Hegel and Negation?* Edited by Audun Mortensen. Cambridge: MIT Press, 2014.